Better Homes and Gardens®

GUIDE TO ENTERTAINING

A party atmosphere, a gracious hostess—entertaining at its best.

BETTER HOMES AND GARDENS BOOKS
Editorial Director: Don Dooley. Managing Editor: Malcolm E. Robinson. Art Director: John Berg
Asst. Managing Editor: Lawrence D. Clayton. Asst. Art Director: Randall Yontz
Entertainment Editor: Ann Francis. Food Editor: Nancy Morton
Senior Editors: Marie Schulz, Joyce Trollope
Associate Editors: Sharyl Heiken, Rosemary Corsiglia
Assistant Editors: Sandra Mapes, Catherine Penney, Elizabeth Strait, Elizabeth Walter
Designers: Arthur Riser, Harijs Priekulis, Faith Berven

CONTENTS

Hospitality—the key to hostessing

People—the most important ingredient

Good food—a major contributor to the success of your entertaining

The new *Better Homes and Gardens Guide to Entertaining* is designed for you, the hostess, whether you are a novice and need detailed plans on where and how to begin; experienced, and want suggestions for new party ideas; or an in-between hostess who wishes to enlarge her hostessing repertoire. What the editors have tried to do is develop a comprehensive treatment of all elements of entertaining so that you may find the answer to any hostessing problem. You'll find photographs, recipes, table plans, and a host of party ideas.

We gratefully acknowledge our debt for contributions from photographers, and regional editors, from etiquette and home entertaining authority Barbara Taylor Bradford, and from many party equipment and home furnishings manufacturers who have given their ideas.

A pretty setting—important to the festive party atmosphere

The daring and unusual combine to make a unique party setting

Who wants or needs a book about entertaining? The hostess who believes that she must show consideration for her guests—the hostess who accepts that the guest's enjoyment is more important than her own—the one who wants her family and friends and her husband's business acquaintances to accept her as a thoughtful, considerate, imaginative hostess—she is the one who wants a guide to entertaining. We hope that person is you.

The emphasis on hostessing is an important part of the American scene. We hope, too, that you're one who is enjoying this phase of American life and that you want new ideas and common sense ideas to make your entertaining a little more special, a little easier.

The goal of *Guide to Entertaining* is to help you enjoy being a hostess—to help you enjoy your own party through the pleasure of your guests. The rules which are sprinkled throughout the book are for guidance. By observing them, you will have the time and ease of mind to enjoy the party yourself.

But, to fulfill your role of hostess you must understand the basics of entertaining. Often in entertaining we forget the small details which can ensure our guests comfort and pleasure. This is where a guide to entertaining enters. It can give you new approaches and new ideas in giving parties yet guide you in the rules of the old.

The guidebook is not geared only to the beginning hostess. It caters, too, to the old-timers, the in-betweeners, and to all who want more ideas and how-to's besides the fundamentals of entertaining and etiquette. It caters to all who want to be a good hostess.

The way to be the hostess you'd like to be is to practice. Give simple, beautifully arranged parties for a few and add to your party repertoire as you gain confidence and knowledge. Learn the short-cut tricks and when to use them. Learn what you can do to your surroundings to dress them up for a party. Learn what meals or snacks you prepare best and which are appropriate for the different occasions. Do everything that will make you confident of your hostessing ability.

And the nicest thing about practicing is that you're entertaining and being with people you enjoy, and you are becoming a gracious hostess.

You'll learn all the tricks and secrets and what is required in making a party a success by giving parties. You'll learn that your guests are the most important ingredient. They are the ones you want to please and are the main reason the party exists. And you'll discover that what you serve is important, for at every gathering, large or small, refreshments are a standard part of the plan. The menu can be simple or elaborate, but chances are that in either case it is dressed up in its party best. How the guests are entertained is also important. Whether it's an afternoon of swimming and boating or an evening of conversation, what your guests enjoy doing and how they respond to what you have planned is an important element in a successful party.

Decorations and accessories, too, help set a party atmosphere. Little touches here and there, such as elaborately contrived banners and balloons, can be equally effective in saying "this is special, just for you." And the element that holds this all together is the mood you, the hostess, create. When there is a feeling of a good-time-about-to-happen, when there is a feeling of warmth and of welcome, your guests will pick up the mood and help you make your entertaining a success.

Guide to Entertaining sets out to help the hostess balance these elements together. It is organized as your approach to giving a party might be.

The first chapter starts with the beginnings of entertaining—the planning. Here you'll learn how to put the party together; how many to invite; how to keep records which help you with future entertaining. Then come the party themes—ideas you can adapt to any kind of party you want to give. "Any-time-Party Time" is devoted to explaining the time-of-day occasions (brunch, lunch, and tea through late-night supper) including invitations, menus, and entertainment. Special occasions arise in everyone's lives and deserve recognition.

Party furnishings add convenience to entertaining

Table settings help set the atmosphere and theme.

Chapter IV, "Special Occasions," describes ways to celebrate adult's and children's birthdays, wedding and baby showers, anniversaries, housewarmings, bon voyage parties, and teen special events, and Chapter V, "Holidays," describes ways to celebrate the special days of the year from New Year's Day through Christmas. Occasionally, the hostess is called on to entertain in an emergency or unusual situation. This special situation entertaining may be entertaining in limited space, giving a party in a hurry, entertaining on a budget, or entertaining away from home. These are covered in "Special Situation Entertaining."

The next chapter, "Table Settings and Centerpieces," explains the how-to's of setting formal and informal tables, dinner, lunch, and buffet table and of party centerpieces. Chapter VIII is the chapter on party etiquette. It is basic and fundamental—a refresher course of the common-sense rules of behavior. The

chapter on party games gives samples, some rules, and the many kinds of party entertainment available for those of you who enjoy organizing a gathering of game-fans.

In many of the chapters, those dealing with specific parties, there are complete menu suggestions. Many of the recipes in the menu suggestions are starred, and the complete recipe can be found in Chapter X. Also included in this last chapter are a chart of how-to-plan food for a crowd, a wine guide, wine and cocktail recipes, and a list of useful party equipment.

This, then, is our Guide to Entertaining: a guide, not a rule book, to entertaining since so few situations in entertaining are ever exactly alike. We hope you will find it a useful tool in your capacity as the gracious hostess and that you will find pleasure in reading it, in trying the recipes, and in practicing the guides suggested by it.

Colorful decorations set a party theme and lend festivity.

PLANNING A PARTY

Giving a party should be fun, and it can be if you plan down to the last detail. The experienced hostess will have an established party planning method. She will know the shortcuts, the rules, and the advantages of the party plan.

What are the advantages? The foremost is a successful party given by a relaxed and confident hostess. By budgeting her time wisely and giving the proper attention to each detail, she'll have saved herself money (she shops early and wisely and does many of the things herself), time (a little bit each day adds up to hours saved the day of the party), energy (she'll be relaxed), and potential calamities (she's cleverly avoided them).

That kind of success and planning takes practice and if you have not had years of party-giving experience, this chapter may be able to help you with some of the fundamentals of successful party plan-

ning. We've drawn all of the elements that go into planning and preparing for a party together to help start you on your way.

How many and who you invite is first on the list. Then the party generals of where, when, and what type are determined. Next are the specific plans within the plans—depending on the first considerations, how do you select the menu? choose the entertainment? the decorations? and accessories? The last details, but by no means the least important, are how to schedule the events, keep party records, and save yourself valuable time.

No plan can be perfect without an optimistic, cheerful hostess arranging them and passing her happy mood on to her guests. The most elegant setting and menu you can concoct will fall flat unless you, the hostess, are relaxed and happy —the most important elements in any party plan.

←**Special decorations,** a festively set table, and a generous amount of food ready to be served, make this party setting inviting to everyone. It takes careful planning to have your house party-perfect before guests arrive and food all prepared, ready to serve at the same time and a wise hostess has a plan.

How many to invite

As a starting point, decide how many you'd like to invite. The number of guests will be one of the first determining factors of the type of party you give, of what you serve, and where. So a tentative guest list needs to be decided early in your planning.

The number you invite will depend on three factors: The capacity of your home, how many you feel capable of handling smoothly, and your purpose or reason for giving the party.

Beginning with the capacity factor, you are limited only by the number of chairs, floor cushions, sofas, and benches you have. For dining, the same holds true. The number of chairs you have and can fit around your table is your guide. Some hostesses don't mind rearranging or storing their furniture to make room for more guests. This is one solution to fitting in more people than you could otherwise, if you don't object to disturbing the room's decor.

But numbers for parties held out of doors can be a bit more flexible than for those held inside, although you still must consider some form of seating arrangements for all.

Above all, experience will tell you how many you can entertain. Until you've reached that point of party-giving and knowing experience, you'll need to estimate and try handling different size crowds. The number your house holds comfortably is your best guide.

If you have help, permanently or for just the party day, you can handle more than you can alone.

The intent, or occasion, dictates the number of guests also. For an evening of good conversation, you'll probably want to limit the number of guests to fewer than ten. Add one or two and you have a good grouping for introducing a newcomer to your friends or for an evening of party games. And for an open house honoring a 50th anniversary celebration you'll probably want to invite even more than your home can

The potluck adapts easily to large crowds when everyone has a part in the preparations. It's perfect for a neighborhood gathering, church socials, or meetings of the couples club. Each couple brings one dish, sometimes suggested by the hostess, so that no one person has too much to do. The combinations are often a pleasant surprise and result in plans for more potluck parties.

An elegant dinner party is a pleasant way to → entertain a few friends for an evening. The cozy atmosphere, the carefully and imaginatively set table, and the thoughtfully planned menu are conducive to stimulating conversation. A pleasant way to end the evening is with coffee and dessert served in the living room, where the hostess serves the coffee, hot and fresh, from the coffee table.

Garden lunches and brunches in the sunshine have a casual air about them that makes guests happy they have come to your home. Carry out the garden colors in the scheme of your table setting to add a special note to the party.

A cheerful kitchen doubles as a party room when the mood is right and when you need the space. You can help set the mood by selecting accessories that change your room from its everyday dress to its party apparel.

hold so stagger the invitation hours. Those between dinner-party size and large-party size numbers can be awkward to handle if the guests do not know each other. Numbers between 12 and 20 are often too large for a single conversation and too small to break comfortably into smaller groups. Getting this number range to mix will often tax your knowledge as a hostess.

"*Who*" *makes the party*

Who to invite is a very important consideration. The right blend of guests can make the evening sparkle. The wrong mixture will make it flat.

Learning how to mix personalities is an art that must be practiced. There are a few guidelines, however, which may be able to help the beginner.

First think about the interests of those you'd like to invite. Often you invite friends who know each other. Then you don't really need to worry. However, there are times when you want to visit with those you don't know well, and you want them to meet some of your other acquaintances. The first thing to consider is the shared interests of the guests. If there is one bond between couples there will be at least one topic on which to converse.

Consider also, the occupations of the people. A mixture of professions is more interesting than having all in one field. You'll end up listening to an evening of shoptalk when everyone is employed by the same or similar firms.

Some talkers and some listeners help make a compatible group—if the talkers do not deliver monologues and the listeners do contribute a little to the conversation. Try for a blend of happily active participants in both areas of talking and listening.

To get this mixture it is often wise to invite at least a few people who already know each other. They can start the chatter and draw others into their conversation. When no one knows anyone but the host or hostess, it places too much of a burden on that couple who must be tending to other duties also throughout the party.

Age is another factor. Don't be afraid to mix age groups, unless the situation prohibits it (a party revolving around touch football would be inappropriate for your elderly friends). Compatibility lies in common interests of people more than in common ages.

You will find guest lists for large gatherings are easier to handle than for small. If you plan some talkers and some listeners, and a variety of professions and interests, you can leave the guests to move from group to group until they find the most compatible one.

But what about inviting those you "owe" an invitation? Try to choose a party at which they would enjoy themselves remembering not to get all of your obligations out of the way in one mass affair (unless you're sure everyone will enjoy themselves). If one couple does not mix well in a crowd and would prefer a small dinner party, give one for them. You owe them that consideration as their hostess.

But do not make things hard on yourself by inviting those you do not like. If it is impossible not to invite them, include those people in a large party so you won't be forced to be unnaturally pleasant all through the party.

Finally, when you are planning a party for a guest of honor, plan the guest list for that person. This time consider his friends rather than yours. Then, if the occasion permits, add some friends of yours who, you think, he might enjoy meeting.

Where to hold the party

Anywhere you have space is appropriate for gathering people. Even if the setting doesn't seem ideal to you, no one will care if the hospitality is warm and if it is a time of fun and relaxation.

The question of where? may already be answered by how many? and who are coming? but the settings can vary for the various types of party. A luncheon can be as much fun in the kitchen or on the patio as in a formal dining room. The family room is as perfect for cocktail parties as it is for brunches or late supper parties. You can even decorate the garage, carport, or attic, for parties if you wish.

Imagination in the setting of your party might be the novelty you've been looking for to set the event apart. You can use a barn, a boat, a meadow, your garage, or the stage of your local theater—anywhere that there is space can be made into a party site. Just be sure that everything you need is available or can be taken to the spot.

Don't let the setting worry you. As long as there is room for your guests to gather, to converse, and to feast on your specialties, the setting will not seem important.

What kind of party?

The kind of party you give will be determined by certain factors: the number of people you'd like to invite and who; when and where you intend to hold the party; what you do and like the best; and the resources you have available or can obtain.

The number of guests you have decided to invite, will, in a great part, determine the type of party you give. For six or eight you could easily give a dinner party. For a few more, perhaps a buffet supper would be easier. For large numbers, snacks of appetizers at an open house or cocktail party would be a logical choice. You have many choices of kinds of parties to give for the many ranges of numbers of guests.

Whom you invite is another determining factor. What those who are invited enjoy should be considered—and who is invited depends on the type of party you plan. If you're planning to invite older guests, you won't give a sit-on-the-grass barbecue. So consider ages, interests, and favorites of those you're inviting when you plan your party.

A major determinant to the kind of party you select is when it will be held. Certain parties are appropriate at only certain times of the day. If you're planning a midmorning gathering, it will be either a brunch or a coffee. A noon-time function will be a luncheon. Your decision will be how to arrange the party within the limits set by the time

of day. Will it be a buffet or sit-down brunch? That decision will depend on the factors previously mentioned.

Another factor in deciding what kind of party to give is where you plan to have the party. You'll have a different choice if it's to be in your dining room than if you're planning to hold the party in a nearby park. The facilities that are available to you will make one kind of party easier and more logical than another kind of party.

You are the most important deciding element. What do you like to do best in entertaining? Is your forte the dinner party for six? the afternoon tea? the informal, midmorning brunch? or a cocktail party for 100? Perhaps you feel you can easily handle two or three of these types. Whatever party you consider the easiest should be a major factor.

What you have available in the way of resources—space, party equipment, budget, help, now enters the picture.

If your space is limited, a small dinner party or a tea in which the hours are staggered might be the answer. If you have access to an outdoor area, you can enlarge your space and guest list. For those fortunate enough to have unlimited space, the types of parties they can give can also be unlimited.

Extra party equipment can be rented if you'd like to give a party and don't have all that is necessary. You can also plan a party such as a potluck in which guests help by bringing one piece of equipment and one part of the meal along with them. While what you have available in the way of dining facilities will help determine whether or not you can give a luncheon or a dinner, party equipment is always available from one source or another. You can make substitutions, if necessary, so don't let that be the soul basis for the kind of party you choose to give.

Your budget and how you use it will be an important item. This will determine if it's to be a hot dog barbecue or a caviar and tenderloin dinner. You can be creative on a limited budget, however. Choose what you do best, and it can become exquisite party fare. Do plan within your budget, because you

Compliments are in store for you when you serve a nutritious, attractive, and delicious meal. It's easy to achieve the well-balanced menu by following the meal planning guides set up by nutrition experts. Select a food from each of the four basic groups—milk group, meat group, vegetable-fruit group, and bread-cereal group. Then add the extras as desired (butter, sugar, increased servings).

By following six easy steps, you can plan your party menu with the assurance that it will be valuable as well as festive. First select a main dish which will provide each person with one serving of meat, fish, or poultry. Add a bread or cereal prod-

uct which will complement the main dish. Next, select a vegetable to serve either hot or cold. Add another complement in the way of a fruit or vegetable salad. Then top off the meal with the appropriate dessert and beverage.

Mealtime should be relaxing and it is, if you sit down to an unhurried, attractive meal. Consider yourself an artist painting a picture. The table setting is the background and the meal is the center of focus. Together they create an atmosphere which influences the appetite of your guests. The colorful, eye-appealing meal in the photograph below exemplifies this pleasing picture.

won't enjoy your own party if you're feeling guilty about the expense. But let your imagination keep the party fare from looking sparse and the atmosphere one of worry and apprehension.

Your party selection is increased when you have extra help. If you're able to hire someone, either one helper or an entire catering service, you can consider more formal affairs: a dinner-dance, a formal dinner, or a cocktail party for several hundred guests. One helper is often sufficient and it is worth considering hiring someone when you want to arrange a party you feel might be more than you could do alone.

What to serve

The first consideration of what to serve is the type of party you're giving. If it's a luncheon, you'll want a light luncheon menu; if it's an open house you'll want an easy-to-serve, easy-to-eat snack menu. If it's a dinner, you'll want a substantial dinner menu. In the same line, the time of day will be a point to consider—if you're giving a midmorning brunch, a noon luncheon, an early supper, or a late-night dinner.

Who you've invited is important. A party of all women will require a different plan for food than if men were invited. For some guests you might like to fix a more elaborate fare than for others. Perhaps a friend of yours has a favorite among your party dishes. You can serve that to let him know he's special. Also you'll need to consider who is coming if your party is on a Friday or if you've invited foreign guests—their religion will often determine what they can eat. These are considerations that make you a successful hostess.

Numbers, too, will enter your planning. For a large crowd it is best to stick to standards and dishes that will keep their flavor and temperature throughout the dinner or evening. For smaller numbers you can be a bit more exotic in your choices (just remember to experiment on your family first).

Almost every hostess has a specialty, or one or two dishes she enjoys fixing more than any others. That specialty, whether it is an appetizer or a main dish, will be safe and welcome. It also gives the hostess extra confidence that what she is serving is the best. An aid in this area is a party notebook with guests' favorites noted. The notebook will help make selection easier and remind the hostess of what she has served before and how it was received.

Since you've invited people you like to be with, don't select foods that take a great preparation time. To let you spend as much time as possible with your guests, and to keep you from scurrying around in the kitchen until the very last minute before the guests arrive, try to select foods that can be prepared beforehand or that take little care during the party. If you do have help, the amount of preparation time won't be as much of a determining factor. Do be sure, however, that the help knows how soon to start the preparations and when to serve the food.

Standard meal planning guides should also be your guides. Select the main dish first, then choose the accompaniments considering color, texture, temperature, and flavor. A variety makes a meal more appetizing. Plan some light and some heavier dishes also, varying from course to course.

Standard meal guides list the courses which make up the various meals. Breakfast or brunch menus usually consist of an egg dish accompanied by a meat or fish, a bread or toast, a fruit or fruit juice, jams, jellies, and coffee, hot chocolate, or milk.

The luncheon menu calls for a light main dish-casserole, salad, or special sandwich—a vegetable, a bread, light dessert, and beverage.

For a small tea or the tea reception, the menu size will vary. Two or three types of sandwiches and perhaps a cake is sufficient for the small tea. Four or five types of sandwiches, and two or three types of sweets plus mints and nuts accompany the tea and coffee at a large tea reception.

Dinner menus usually consist of a main dish, a starchy vegetable, a green or yellow vegetable, a salad, dessert, bread, and beverage. The appetizer can be a part of the meal as the first course or an extra before the meal.

Quantities and weights of the various menus depend on your plans and on guest appetites.

For snack parties keep variety in mind. If possible serve both hot and cold snacks. Vary the textures, colors, and tastes. Choose also by the appearance of the finished food. The buffet or cocktail table should look as appetizing as a well appointed dinner table.

Ideas for party foods are everywhere. Cook books are abundant. Every party giver should have one large basic cook book. Home service magazines contain party and recipe suggestions in almost every issue. You can easily expand your party menu repertoire with these aids and make party-giving more fun for you and your guests.

Scheduling events

Even the veteran party-giver finds a schedule of events helpful because each party is different. A written timetable can save you invaluable time and countless steps. When your plans are formulated, record each detail that must be attended to—from sending the invitations to greeting your guests at the door. You'll find such a listing extremely helpful and you'll be less likely to forget last-minute items.

Your first thought will be for the date you have scheduled the party—on the weekend or during the week. Hopefully you've set the date for a time most convenient for you so that you will have adequate time to prepare.

Another important first thought will be whether you will be arranging the party yourself or have help. With help, much of the preparation can be scheduled for a later time than without help. As soon as the date of the party is definite, make all the necessary arrangements to hire the help.

To determine how to allot your time for the remainder of the items, turn to your party notebook. Refresh your memory on how you arrange schedules and how to improve those schedules for this party. Another helpful aid is an inventory of party equipment. You can see at a glance what you have and what you need for entertaining this time.

Your guest list should already be determined. Schedule now the time to send the invitations. Next decide on your menu and when to buy the staples and when to buy the perishables. Allow several days before the party for ordering and picking up the specialties such as flowers and unusual foods. Do your heavy housecleaning then, too.

The day before the party pick up the food you'll need and prepare any do-ahead dishes you can. See that your tableware is clean, your tablecloth ironed, and any special equipment running smoothly. You might clear out the coat closet of family coats and make sure you have plenty of hangers.

On the day of the party finish preparing any food that can be done early, check the house for dust, put out fresh towels and guest accessories in the bathroom, set your table or sideboard,

---

Thursday for fondue supper

order flowers
call meat shop
clean house

Friday

buy groceries
buy fuel for burner
freeze extra ice
make dips and spreads
make dessert
press tablecloth
press hostess pants

Saturday

Morning
pick up meat
wash and store salad greens
clean silver
arrange centerpiece
Afternoon
dust
set table
arrange canapes
put fresh towels in guest bath
rest

Inexpensive, yet colorful and fun, decorations for your table can set your party mood and establish the theme. Red, white, and blue provides an appropriate color theme for any patriotic holiday—Independence Day, George Washington's birthday, Veteran's Day, and Armed Forces Day. These corrugated cardboard innovations are easy to make and easy on the budget. Use blue-painted cardboard for place mats and trim with gold, red, white, and blue ribbon. Trim tubes of corrugated paper with ribbon for napkin rings. For the centerpiece, cover a coffee can with corrugated board. Cut two- by four-inch strips of cardboard and fold back for the abstract flower. Center with a large gold tree ornament. Glue plastic cups together and trim with starburst for the finale.

A **"Last Night to Crow"** party table designates the end of the old year. It's a variation on an old theme that takes on a new look. With imagination, you can make your decorations have a new look, too. Browse through gift shops and look through idea magazines to give your creativity a start. Then inventory what you have, add to your party stock if necessary, and design your own original and clever party sets.

The elements used in this setting are a red burlap tablecloth bordered with ball fringe, an inverted wicker basket stand for the rooster candle cover of wrought iron, an arrangement of magnolia leaves, milo corn heads, Italian wheat, and candles.

and relax. Try to save at least an hour for yourself to rest and get ready before any last minute details or before the guests arrive. The sample schedule on page 19 is to let you see how one hostess plans for her party preparations.

Selecting decorations

Decorating for a party, whether you simply place fresh flowers around the room or elaborately fill the room with balloons, is important in presenting a party atmosphere. Special adornments show that you think this is a special occasion and they help put your guests in a festive mood. The time to decorate is optional, whenever it is appropriate and whenever you want to.

The degree to which you decorate depends on the party. It is fun occasionally to go all out in decorating for theme parties, birthday parties, or holiday parties. Everything can be coordinated from the menu to the wall hangings. For children's parties the decorations are especially important. They are what the little guests remember and what makes a party right for them.

You can decorate simply or elaborately. The simple decorating includes the minimum—a clean house, a centerpiece, and well chosen and placed accessories. The elaborate includes changing or disguising your party room with adornments—covering the ceiling with paper balls, hanging fishnets on walls, placing seashells all around the room.

It is probably easiest to decorate from what you have available. If you don't have just the right thing, there are scores of sources to make the right purchase—variety stores, discount stores, junk shops, specialty shops, and neighborhood garage sales. If the man of the house is a handyman, he can make appropriate decorations in his workshop. Do be sure to plan according to the tastes of your guests. If some would feel uncomfortable in an elaborately contrived Hawaiian atmosphere, decorate by suggestion instead. A touch here and there, in the ashtrays, the centerpiece, and food might be enough.

Ashtrays, centerpieces, cigarette box-es, floor cushions, and candles come under the heading of accessories. They're the items necessary for any party. Accessories in the right color and mood can be your entire decorating scheme. Perhaps the most important part of any party decorating is a sparkling clean house. It says that you've done your best for your guests—even as much as a houseful of colorful balloons—and that they are indeed special.

How to entertain guests

Entertainment at parties can range from hiring professional musicians or playing card games, to engaging solely in conversation. Some parties call for elaborate forms of entertainment—a style show benefit, a dinner-dance. Others call for more simplified entertainment—a fondue supper, a baby shower, or a barbecue. In some the form of entertainment is "built-in" and in others it is "brought in."

A "built-in" need not be elaborate. It might revolve around a family game room or a swimming pool. It might stem from a conversation, or from a particular guest. But it is not contrived.

A "brought-in" is as its name implies —something specifically brought in to help the event. When considering bringing in some form of entertainment, think first of your guests and choose what they most enjoy. It would be cruel to subject unwilling participants to an evening of charades and other party games. On the other hand, some people enjoy party games and could think of no more fun way to spend an evening.

There are countless possibilities of things to do at parties. Party games are manufactured specifically for this purpose. There are outdoor activities such as boating and swimming and attending spectator sports and there are indoor activities such as table tennis and pool. You can even gather a group to watch a television special.

If you do plan your party around an activity, be sure to let your guests know when you issue the invitations. Then if the idea does not appeal to them, they have a chance to decline.

Party records

You'll find a party notebook an invaluable aid in planning, especially if you entertain frequently. It can be in any form you choose—in a loose-leaf notebook, a spiral notebook, or one printed especially for the purpose. It will be a great time-saver for you and worth the minutes it takes to record the details. The notebook can hold any information you think helpful. It can remind you of how you organized the party and your time; what equipment was used; the table setting; and the help that was hired. You can jot down where the party was held, who was invited, accepted, and came. And what food was served and how. You can even include a section on your party clothes and on guest likes and dislikes. The chart illustrated is to give you a start. As you entertain more you'll probably add new headings for information and comments to fit your own style of entertaining.

Things to know

There are little conveniences and necessities that every hostess should know—things to make her job easier and make her a "professional." For the beginning hostess a guide to buying and using dinnerware and glassware will be an invaluable aid. For all hostesses, hints on preparing for and cleaning up after a party will be more than helpful.

Dinnerware

What is a basic table wardrobe? This is a question asked by every woman faced with making a selection of tableware.

Two sets of dishes are advised. You'll probably want to select one pattern in fine china for special occasions and one in a more casual pattern for everyday use. If your budget dictates one set to begin with, consider a plain white or off-white dish that has easy-care properties but looks elegant.

Six place settings are a good goal for your first dinnerware. Usually a young couple will entertain only one or two other couples. More place settings can be added in time.

Five-piece place settings are most common. This includes a dinner plate, dessert or salad plate, a butter plate, a cup and saucer. Soup dishes would probably be the next item you'd want to add to your dinnerware and then fruit bowls.

Party: Date:	Time:
Guest list: Hostess wore: Entertainment:	Menu: Decorations:
Comments:	

It's also nice to start with some basic serving pieces—bowls and platters.

In silverware, you'll need only as many place settings as you have of china. A basic four-piece place setting will include a dinner fork, salad fork, place knife, and teaspoon. With a five-piece, you'll receive the soup spoon; with a six piece, the butter spreader.

How to select dinnerware

When you're picking dinnerware, consider these things: *Suitability*—the type and pattern of your dinnerware should suit your way of life and your plans for entertaining. Is the ware compatible with the style of your furnishings? Think about the way you like your coffee and remember coffee will cool more quickly in a cup with a wide opening. Examine tableware piece by piece to see if you would be satisfied with it for comfort and ease of handling as well as eye appeal. *Durability*—your dinnerware should require a minimum of coddling. Determine how break-resistant it is. Look for imperfections. How easily will it chip and, if chipped, will it absorb grease and food? Be sure of the decorations. You don't want them to wear off, fade, or discolor. It should be washable in standard household soaps and detergents. *Availability*—it's better to choose a pattern from open stock so that replacements can be made if breakage is a problem or if you're planning additions. If the pattern should be taken off the market, it's helpful if it is such that you can find suitable replacements in a harmonious design, color, and shape. *Pattern and color*—will food look appetizing on it? A pattern should be far enough from the edge so that if chipping occurs, the chips won't break into the color conspicuously. Also, be sure the pattern is not one you'll tire of. *Design and shape*—the shapes of the various pieces should be pleasing and practical, and the dishes should be easy to handle. The two basic plate shapes are coupe and rim—decide which you prefer. The cup should balance well and should not tip whether filled or empty. Make sure the cup handle is attached firmly and is comfortable to hold.

Cost—is the cost in line with the use you anticipate giving the dinnerware? The enjoyment of the dinnerware and the expected life of your choice should balance the price you expect to pay.

Care of dinnerware

Here are care instructions for the four common types of dinnerwares.
Glass-ceramic: This type is completely dishwasher-proof—even the patterns with metallic bandings. Detergents won't harm its finish and decorations won't wash off. Glass-ceramic dinnerware needs no special care and these dishes may be stacked one on top of the other in your cupboard with no special pads between for protection.
Melamine or plastic dinnerware: This ware falls into the same easy and automatic care classification as glass-ceramic. Melamine dishes can be safely washed in a dishwasher. But don't scrub the surface with cleaning pads.
Fine china: This has amazing durability despite its fragile appearance. Washing instructions are simple: (1) Rinse china with a soft brush or wiper. (2) Don't let coffee dry in cups. (3) When washing by hand, use whatever mild soap or detergent you prefer. (4) If you're using an automatic dishwasher, be sure your plates are properly loaded so they don't rub up against each other. Use soap or detergent recommended by the manufacturer. When storing, use separating pads.
Ceramics, earthenware, ironstone: All should be washed in the same manner as fine china. Some hand-painted dinnerware that has been improperly fired will not withstand any vigorous washing. If you have any questions about any particular type of dinnerware, consult the manufacturer about the proper care.

Glassware

Glassware has a charm no well-dressed table should be without. Choose yours carefully to complement your china, your silver, and your room decor.

Glassware will depend on your way of living. If you have melamine or other informal dishes, for everyday, you may want to select unbreakable dishwasher-proof plastic tumblers. It's nice to have more glasses on hand than your dinnerware place settings since very often guests are only served beverages and not a complete meal.

You will need only as many crystal settings as you have fine china. If you're purchasing crystal a piece at a time, start with the water goblets, then add sherbets, and last, wines.

The basic place setting for stemware is goblet, sherbet, juice, iced tea, and seven- or eight-inch liner plate. The basic beverage place setting for bar or tableware is water, juice, old-fashioned, highball, pilsner, and whiskey sour.

The how-to of choosing glassware includes looking and listening. Look for beauty in the material itself. Clear crystal has the look of a fine diamond. Glass coloring is done with chemicals. Look for a rich and sparkling luster. Listen by tapping the rim of the goblet with your fingernail while you hold the footed base. A bell-like tone is what you should hear. It's the ring of strength and lasting brilliancy.

The best stemware has graceful proportions. There are seven basic shapes you'll find on store shelves: (1) bucket; (2) flared; (3) cylindrical; (4) spherical; (5) tulip; (6) conical; (7) bell.

Stemmed goblets bring grace to the table. But sometimes they're a hazard, too. Check the base for proportionate breadth and weight before you buy.

There are 11 popular sizes of glasses in a stemware pattern: (1) 11 oz. water or milk goblet; (2) 7 oz. high sherbet; (3) 7 oz. low sherbet (and wine); (4) 6 oz. parfait—can also be used for whiskey sour or pilsner; (5) 4 oz. cocktail; (6) 5 oz. claret for red wines; (7) 4 oz. wine or brandies; (8) 1 oz. liqueur cordial; (9) 4½ oz. oyster cocktail; (10) 15 oz. luncheon goblet; (11) 5 oz. juice. In addition, there is usually a dessert finger bowl, and 7- and 8-inch plates for salad, cake, or liner plates.

Party games can help turn tongue-tied guests into light-hearted contestants. New games are being manufactured each year and are geared to every taste and age. Some require guile and concentration, others manual dexterity, still others a way with words. This game, called Tangle, is a game of concentration, perfect for a quiet afternoon after an early luncheon party.

Unfooted beverage sets come in six sizes: (1) 7½ oz. old-fashioned cocktail and sodas; (2) 12 oz. double old-fashioned; (3) 12 oz. highball, milk, water, ice cream sodas, and soft drinks; (4) 9 oz. scotch and soda—doubles for iced tea; (5) 5 oz. whiskey sour or short cocktails; (6) 1½ oz. whiskey.

The care of glassware is as important as its selection. Use mild suds and warm water for washing; never caustic powders. A few drops of bluing will add luster. Rinse in cool water and drain. Polish gently, holding onto the bowl part of the goblet. Use a lint-free towel.

Avoid sudden temperature changes. Extreme heat causes glass to expand; cold causes it to contract. Both result in cracking.

Glasses inadvertently piled inside each other sometimes stick together. Fill the inside glass with cold water and immerse the outer one in warm.

Before you decide about trusting your delicate crystal to your dishwasher, check with the dishwasher manufacturer, or the store where you made the crystal purchase. You must be especially careful if your crystal has platinum, gold, or enameled bands.

Always store your crystal right side up, and, as you're putting it away, check for nicks. If you find any nicks, you can repair with care by using 00 emery paper wrapped around a blunt tool. This filing will make a frosted edge which you can touch up with polishing rouge on a leather strap. Rub gently in both operations.

Hostess Hints

There are many housekeeping tricks that simplify the before and after of entertaining. Proper care and storage of party linens will be one of the hostesses best time-savers.

Remove creases in table linens right on the table. Place a bath towel, folded in thirds, on top of the table. Open the cloth, place creased area on the towel. No need to predampen; press spray button on steam iron and creases disappear.

Store linens such as mats, table runners, and small cloths by rolling them on a mailing tube, sawed-off broom handle, or cardboard shelf-paper tube. For prolonged storage (used once a year or less) launder the linens and store without starching and ironing.

If the party has left a stain on your best tablecloth—or if some of your linens are simply showing their age—revive them with these tricks.

First, act fast on stains. You can't attack the stain while the party is in progress, but the sooner you do go to work on it, the easier it is to remove. Before any of your linens are laundered, you should pretreat and remove stains.

For candle wax, start by scraping as much wax as possible off the fabric. To remove remaining wax, place fabric between blotters or paper towels, then press with a warm iron. If spot remains, sponge with grease solvent (trichloroethane). If fabric permits, pour boiling water through spot, or bleach.

For greasy stains (ice cream, butter, milk, salad dressings), sponge or soak fabric in cold water. Rub detergent into spot and launder. Sponge, with grease solvent; bleach if fabric permits.

Coffee and tea stains can usually be removed in hot, soapy water. Bleach if stain remains and fabric permits.

Color therapy—right now (after removing stains) is the time to think about giving your linens a bright new look with dye. Many colors are available in the new liquid form. But first, check your automatic washer care-and-use book to see if your appliance can be used for this special job. If no instructions are available, try these: Use the hottest water available. Set for regular, hot wash/cold rinse cycle. Add the dye solution. Agitate briefly to mix. Place clean, wet article in machine, unfolded. Check final rinse to see if color remains. A second rinse may be needed. Clean machine by running through regular cycle with detergent and one-fourth cup of bleach. Wipe out with damp cloth to remove any sign of color.

For more change, add new bright, colorful fringes and braids. Spray starches and sizing make ironing easier and enhance the looks and feel of the finished product.

PARTY THEMES

When do you use a theme for a party? Anytime you give one if you'd like. It may be a birthday, a holiday, a baby shower, an after-theatre dinner—the event or reason is your theme. The parties in this chapter, however, are not the usual themes. They're the special ones, the ones you dream up when you want to give your party an unusual or exciting touch.

These party themes can be used for any of the usual parties—for banquets, and barbecues, for no reason at all other than you're in a mood to give a party—and an unusual one at that. They're beautiful, they're fun, and they challenge your own ingenuity and creativity.

And by having a central theme, you extend life to your party by adding color and excitement. This makes planning and giving the party all the more fun for you, and will ensure your guests a party time they'll remember for a long while.

The chapter on party themes is divided by main areas—activity themes, season themes, regions of the United States themes, foreign country themes, and ages or time themes. Under each main area are listed ideas that fit that area. For an "activity party" you can plan a cook-at-the-table affair or a play-and-buffet evening (play games and serve a buffet-style supper or snacks). Hopefully, you'll be able to adapt any or all of the ideas to your home and your area. If the theme calls for a beach picnic atmosphere, and there's no beach nearby, improvise by turning your family room or patio into a sand and surf setting. If you don't have all the equipment that's called for, use your imagination to dream up substitutions. The main purpose of the chapter is to give you the idea and a few of the details and let you take over from there. Perhaps you'll find an even better idea of your own on the way.

← **Travel to Mexico** the easy way—stay in your own home and bring Mexico to you. Guests will delight at the colorful theme and the hearty menu from south-of-the-border. For decorations find casual pottery, bright scarves, tablecloths, napkins, Mexican tinware, and a pinata to break after dinner.

ACTIVITY THEMES

Plan a theme around an activity and entertain guests by letting them entertain themselves. "Cook-at-the-table" parties are popular and are perfect for a leisurely supper. A "play-and-buffet" party combines an evening of game-playing with the informal buffet supper. At both, your guests amuse themselves with your pre-planned activities.

Cook-at-the-table

Dinner is dramatic and definitely company when your guests cook their own meal right at the table.

The surprise and one of the most pleasant parts of a cook-it-yourself party is that there is a minimum of last-minute fuss. The dishes do require chopping and slicing ahead of time, but the results are worth it.

Chinese Hot Pot* is a meal in itself, perfect to serve six people after the show or for a leisurely evening of dinner and conversation. Slice the food and make the sauces early. When guests are hungry, just heat the broth and set out sauces and raw tidbits—chunks of eggplant, cross-cut strips of sirloin, halved fresh mushrooms, thin slices of eggplant, shelled shrimp. The cooking liquid is chicken broth. Guests drop a few tidbits at one time into the broth with chopsticks, bamboo tongs, or long-handled forks. In a few minutes, they fish them out and dip them into the zesty sauces. Fluffy rice is a perfect accompaniment. As a finale, dash dry sherry into the broth and pass it in no-handle teacups. Skip dessert, or serve fruit sherbet along with hot tea and fortune cookies.

← **For an outdoor party,** the Mongolian cooker is the center of interest at the table. To use it, fill the chimney with charcoal and add charcoal starter. Cover the cooker then light the charcoal. Fill the cooking container with boiling chicken broth. When the broth returns to a simmer, seat the guests. For indoor cook-at-the-table parties, any chafing dish or electric skillet will do.

*recipes on page 152.

Play-and-buffet

An entire evening of party games— that's a popular theme for many party-givers and -goers. Tables of concentration-, chance-, pencil and paper-, and wit-games give guests a choice and the buffet lets them snack when they choose.

A buffet requires little last-minute cooking. Prepare everything ahead and set the buffet at any time during the party. To serve hot dishes, use hot trays, electric casseroles, and chafing dishes to keep foods serving temperature.

Table after table of party games and an attractively set buffet table in the background invite guests to an evening of pleasure. For an easy buffet idea, serve soups kept warm in vacuum bottles along with trays of cold meats and cheeses, relishes, a variety of breads and crackers, and hot coffee. Guests can serve themselves when there is a break in their particular game.

SEASON PARTY THEMES

Season themes are perhaps some of the easiest to plan. Elements and symbols of summer, fall, winter, and spring are usually readily available. And there's no rule that requires you to use a season theme in-season—if it's a blustery January day and you're longing for the warmth of summer, plan a July-in-January party. Season-theme parties are also ideal for heralding the arrival of the new time of year. Celebrate the first official day of spring with the "spring-iest" party you can concoct. You can do it all regardless of the weather outside in your choice of color scheme, your table setting, your menu, and your planned party activities.

Summer

You may not have a beach in your backyard, but you can give a summer beach picnic any time of year with some advance planning. Start by taking all of your picnic supplies out of their off-season storage—the picnic basket, paper plates and cups, wicker or straw accessories, enamel cookware, plastic picnic carrying cases, and a gaily colored tablecloth. You might even put out the grill.

Next, plan your setting. Convert the family room or basement into a seaside resort or beach with lawn furniture, beach umbrellas, travel posters, and your picnic gear.

Your menu depends on the advance planning. When fresh ear corn is in season, blanch it for 3 or 4 minutes, then freeze it. You'll be able to serve roasted corn to your picnic crew. Order fresh fruit that's not in season where you live from a dealer in an area where it is available. You'll need to order several weeks in advance and to state the date by when you need it to insure arrival by party time. Grill steaks, hot dogs, or hamburgers on an indoor grill or on one set up outside or in the garage. Other picnic foods—tomatoes, green peppers, breads, cold drinks—are usually available all year round.

You may not be able to swim or sun, but you can have guests come in beach attire. Then show home movies of your last summer at the shore and let everyone imagine that they're there.

Fall

Nothing is quite as refreshing or as colorful as a fall day. If you miss this season, hurry it along with a fall festival. The color scheme is traditional—reds, golds, and browns. Dried arrangements and artificial leaves keep almost forever, so bring out your autumn bouquets for your festival decorations. The purpose of the festival is to celebrate the harvest, so be sure to have symbols of the plentiful crop (wheat, gourds, milo corn heads) to use as your centerpiece.

Fall fare is also traditional. The fish are biting, apples are in their glorious peak, and so are the pumpkins. Wild game is popular in autumn and turkey with dressing belongs, too, to this season. You can plan your party fare around the foods of fall no matter what the season—all are available either frozen, fresh, or canned.

To make your party a real fall festival, pattern it after the Octoberfest, a festival held in Munich, Germany, every autumn to celebrate the harvest. Serve beer and sausages (knackwurst and bratwurst), along with your fall vegetables and game. Add a few other Octoberfest dishes such as cabbage, coleslaw, pretzels, and apfel strudel.

Informality is the key to this celebration so have everyone come in casual attire. If you have them available, serve the beer in steins and set your feast on an undraped wooden table. Benches, too, to sit on will add a note of authenticity.

To celebrate this season and to keep with the theme, plan your entertainment around polka music, dancing, and singing. You'll be able to find polka records and dancing instructions, and sing-along records with printed song sheets to help lead you in the festivities.

A table set for fall combines the brilliant colors of the season, the falling leaves, red, ripe apples, and proof that the fishing is great when the waters begin to cool and the shadows are lengthening. Even the tablecloth is dressed for autumn with appliques that duplicate the colorful fall leaves.

It's a beach party and what could be more refreshing after a day of swimming and sunning than a summer meal cooked out-of-doors. When dusk settles, light the campfire and start the coals for the steaks and corn on the cob, then sing songs by the fire and feast until the last embers die.

Winter

A winter entertaining theme is an easy one to plan. There are party ideas galore, and winter provides its own decorating ideas that are natural or easy to concoct. The season is an active one for theater and concert-goers and holiday dinner-givers and there are myriads of winter sports that call for a warming-up party afterwards or a snow picnic during the activities.

A hearty, hot dinner on a cold winter's evening is always right for a hungry crowd. Gather your group for a snow-fest party either before or after a community event. Feature the favorites of winter—a crackling fire, snowmen centerpieces, miniature sleds to hold candy and nuts, ice skates dressed in evergreens to hang on the front door, snowflakes of dainty paper hanging from the ceiling and pasted to the windows, snowbirds resting on leafless branches, and a fragrant, glazed baked ham waiting to be eaten. Serve with the ham Pineapple Refresher* with potato chips, Scalloped Potatoes Supreme*, Garden Wheel Salad*, Chutney Dressing*, buttered rolls, Angel Pineapple Torte*, and coffee.

If you're one who enjoys the outdoor winter sports, plan a snow picnic. Gather up your children's sleds, toboggans, and short skis and head for the slopes. Have everyone bring something for a "hot-luck buffet" and ask them to use insulated jugs and chests to keep warm foods warm and cold things from freezing. Paper and plastic dishes, knives, and forks will make cleanup carefree. Don't forget the wood for the bonfire— you'll probably need it.

If you want, assign guests their part of the meal—plan on cups of oyster stew, crackers, Silver-plated Ski-bum dinners* (they're beef and vegetables cooked in foil bags), crisp cold cabbage slaw, stuffed olives and dill pickles, buttered pumpernickel slices, coffee, cocoa, and mulled cider, and apple pie á la Matterhorn (that's á la mode). The bags the dinner is cooked in will keep hands warm—no plates needed. Carry the slaw in a plastic container tucked inside an insulated picnic bag.

*recipes on pages 153, 154.

Spring

Think of spring and newness—new flowers, new buds on trees, the welcome new warmth, new bright colors. And you also think of festivals to welcome the new season. If the occasion arises for you to have a party in the spring, or if you just invent your own occasion, make it a spring festival.

Decorations for your festival can be those from nature. Laden every surface with early flower-and-spring bouquets. If the flowers aren't available yet, make some from crepe paper, egg cartons, or whatever you can find. Then add a few variety-store butterflies and birds. Cover your table with green and add napkins of bright yellow and pink.

One way to celebrate the arrival of spring is with a wine-tasting party. Wine is the traditional beverage of festivals and celebrations and the wine-tasting party is a good way for the novice to learn and the expert to enjoy the many flavors of wines. Choose from six to eight kinds of wine (half of them red and half of them white) and arrange them on your table in order of tasting.

Start with the lightest white wine and progress to the full-bodied red. Serve, also, breads and mild cheeses. To help guests remember their impressions, supply them with paper and pencil. Then finish your evening with coffee and a gaily decorated spring cake.

When the weather turns warm, people begin moving outside for concerts, plays, and sporting events. Whatever the event, take your supper with you and enjoy a spring picnic on the lawn. By starting time, whisk basket and all back to the car. Be sure to take your spring theme with you. Even at a picnic a bouquet of flowers adds to the mood. Bring picnicware in the brightest colors you can find and a few bright candles in tall hurricane glass lanterns.

This picnic can be a glamorous occasion—start with a Chilled Fruit Toddy*, then provide Cold Roast Chicken*, assorted condiments, Curried Picnic Salad*, and salt sticks. For dessert serve Limed-Pineapple-in-the-Shell*, a cheese-and-cracker tray, and coffee.

Flamboyant trimmings bring a mood of spring merriment to a table. Make colorful mats, napkin holders, and coasters out of paper-mache and the fluorescent flowers cut of egg cartons.

To make the mats, cut a 16-inch circle of corrugated cardboard. Glue two-inch squares of newspaper in overlapping layers to the cardboard with white glue. Brush liquid gesso on both sides and edges, let dry, coat again, let dry, then sand and paint. Outline dark areas with India ink and finish with several coats of acrylic clear gloss spray. The coaster is a 3½-inch circle.

For flowers, cut egg-carton cups into flower shapes. Coat with glue and bend some petals outward. After glue dries, paint with poster paints and trim with ink. Spray with clear gloss. Make some flowers from cardboard covered with glue and newspaper. While glue is damp, cut into flower shapes and bend petals into desired shapes. Paint with gesso and dry before applying poster paints.

Your picture-pretty garden is the ideal setting for a luncheon party. The occasion can be any you think of—the garden club meeting, a best-friend's birthday, or just because. The menu should be as light and airy as the setting. Serve a party salad of fresh vegetables and thinly sliced luncheon meat or tuna, or of fresh fruit and cottage cheese. Serve iced drinks, too.

You'll find a roll-around cart an invaluable aid at an outdoor garden party. Wheel out at once all necessary utensils and all courses to save you many trips in and out of the house.

Sound the horn instead of a dinner bell and let → guests help themselves to this mobile menu: Country-style Barbecue Ribs* precooked by gentle simmering, cooled, then reheated; Caraway Skillet Slaw* tossed with hot bacon dressing just before serving; Quick Poppy-onion Loaf* made from refrigerated dinner rolls; and Chocolate Daisy Cupcakes*. If you'd like to be even more ambitious, add a pot of baked beans to warm while the ribs are heating, bowls of chilled relishes, and hot coffee. To save grill space, bring flame-heated chafing dishes and vacuum containers.

OUTDOOR PARTY THEMES

The great outdoors offers you theme after theme possibility. Use your own yard for a garden party or travel to the country for a tailgate picnic. If you're near a lake or ocean, hostess a boat party. Vacation homes or camping trailers and tents can be the site of a mountain-trout party. You can make the outdoor location of your choice the theme for your next party.

Garden party

You'll want your garden in perfect shape if it's to be the center of attraction at a breakfast, luncheon, or dinner party. So be sure you've watered well at least four days before the party, trimmed out weeds and dead flowers, sprayed with insecticides, swept the patio, and freshened your lawn furniture.

Add to your theme with extra touches—special lighting, outdoor floral arrangements, brightly painted baskets for litter. Carry your garden theme into your table setting, too. Repeat flower colors, add a floral centerpiece, and serve a garden-fresh meal garnished with greens and flower blossoms.

Tailgate picnic

Tack a happy ending or beginning onto any outing with a tailgate picnic. Your location can be the prettiest spot you can find. It's a party way to end a day of antiquing or zoo-visiting or begin a day of football watching "live" (parking-lot picnics are becoming a popular sport before the game). Pre-cooked dishes that need only reheating on a portable grill and chilled foods that stay cool and crisp are ideal for this take-along picnic. Just remember to plan carefully so that foods will be served at their tastiest temperatures. Bring sturdy eating equipment that can be thrown away and, although they're not necessary, camp stools or folding chairs are nice additions for everyone's comfort.

recipes on pages 154-155.

Mariner's sea fare

If you own a boat, large or small, or if you rent one for a day, be sure to plan a mariner's party. It's a take-along special. You take everything you need with you and enjoy it at a particular land site or on board the boat (if you have the room). You'll probably want to plan the party for a small crowd since you will have to carry all of the food and a large group may not fit on one craft. Or you may want to plan a sea caravan. Several boatloads of sailors can meet at the appointed spot for their sea feast.

The outdoors provides the party decorations. All you need to supply are the eating utensils, a tablecloth, a blanket or boat pillows to sit on, and the food. Don't forget the necessary extras—a bottle opener, a sharp knife, salt and pepper, serving spoons, matches, a portable grill, if necessary, charcoal, paper, and firewood.

Sailing and swimming will probably supply your main entertainment, but if you have an energetic gang, take along beach balls, a la crosse set, a badminton set, or a deck of cards for the bridge fans. If you're lunching on board, you might want to take just the cards and other nonathletic party games.

Mountain fish-fry

Whether you're a camping addict or a one-day-by-the-stream fan, you can plan a fish fry by a mountain stream that will make your guests your fans.

Invite a group, large or small, to join you at your camping or picnicking site. If it's remote, be sure to provide maps or have the group form a caravan to follow you to the party. While you are enjoying the beauty of your surroundings, the men in the party should be catching the

← **This sea-faring lunch** can come ashore or be feasted on board anytime. Makings for the submarine sandwiches are kept fresh and cold in the boat's ice chest. Each member of the crew slices and layers his own fillings on the big, crusty rolls. The soft drinks are chilled awhile in the freezer at home then packed next to the relishes to keep them crisp and cold.

Freshly caught mountain trout sizzle over the campfire to provide a tempting aroma for all party-goers. Cook these Mountain Rainbow Trout* the fisherman-tested way for best results, then add Potatoes with Chef's Cheese Sauce*.

feast. (Just in case, you'll probably want to have a well-frozen supply of mountain trout stored in your ice chest.)

To insure the success of the feast, you must cook the freshly caught trout the real fisherman's way—with a light cornmeal and flour coating that doesn't overpower the flavor of the catch. Perfect serve-alongs are baked potatoes topped with cheese sauce (start these at least 45 minutes before the fish), relishes kept crisp in the cooler, melon bought on your way to the party and served with a lemon slice and a strawberry, and plenty of hot coffee, and iced beverages kept chilled in the mountain stream.

To serve your mountain meal all you'll need to provide are plates, forks, spoons, and mugs, and napkins. You can carry the make-ahead cheese sauce with you to keep mixing and cooking utensils to a minimum. For those you'll need only the skillet for the fish, a shallow mixing pan, a spatula, a sharp knife, and foil in which to wrap the potatoes.

If you plan to stay past sunset, remind everyone to bring extra sweaters or shirts to keep warm.

*recipes appear on page 155.

REGIONS OF THE U.S.A.

Pick a region of the United States for a party theme. You don't have to live there —bring the region to your home through your decorations and menu. Select those traits which are characteristic of it— those things which come to your mind first when you think of the area. The north has the Great Lakes, cold winters, tall pines, lobsters, clambakes, and cranberries. A Mexican and Indian influence is felt in the southwest in the food and in the sun-colors so often found in the art and homes of the area. It's easy and fun to transport your guests for a few hours to a different part of the country.

Midwest

Take your guests to Chicago, Minneapolis, or Detroit for a theater or concert evening and a semi-formal dinner of stuffed pork chops, sweet potatoes and apples, and many, many cheeses. Or take them to a small Minnesota town for a delightful supper of Norwegian specialties or to Kansas for a Sunday dinner of fried chicken, homemade bread, and potato salad. Dress your home with bouquets of dried wheat and milo corn heads, with travel posters of city skylines or lush, rolling green hills, and of waving wheat fields and rich gold-brown prairies or of sandhills.

The semi-formal dinner, becoming more and more popular as a midwestern form of entertaining, can serve as your starter idea. The Midwest is known as the "Food Basket of the Nation." That can be your theme. Serve everything in abundance, decorate in generous proportions, plan a full evening of entertainment. Foods indigenous of the area are beef and pork, dairy products in every form, an infinite variety of vegetables, and cereal and flour products from fields of wheat, corn, and oats. Your menu should be simple, but hearty. Serve stuffed pork chops, corn on the cob, crisp shredded cabbage and onion rings in a slaw, juicy red tomato slices, ice cream with toppings, and glasses of milk.

South

It is difficult to localize the South for it is so diversified, but a Plantation Breakfast (or Hunt Breakfast) is a popular form of entertaining in Virginia. Even if you don't have the "hunt" to hold prior to your gathering, you can bring the southern flavor to your party with traditional foods and decorations.

Shrimp, in all forms, mint juleps, southern hams, hot breads, grits and gravy are only a few of a great selection of southern foods. For decorations, call on the rich history of the South. Antiques, if available, such as cooking utensils, china, silver, and glassware, and small furnishings lend authenticity. Make floral and fauna arrangements of boxwood, osage oranges, pyracantha, magnolias, and Spanish moss. If they're not available locally, invest in some of the natural-appearing artificial forms. For added fun, ask guests to come dressed for a hunt, then plan your entertainment for whatever is available—a football game, the Orange Bowl Parade on New Year's Day, or just because it's Sunday.

Your hearty midday breakfast, or brunch, menu will be a long remembered favorite if you serve Southern fried chicken, biscuits, hominy grits, spoon bread, watermelon pickles, sliced fresh tomatoes, mushrooms and watercress in sour cream served on toast, ambrosia, scrambled eggs, hot sausage, and hot spiced cider. With such a generous menu, plan to set the table buffet style. Place the punch bowl and coffee service on a nearby table and let guests serve themselves to everything. You'll need only one other meal the day of this feast.

A Plantation Breakfast says "Southern hospitality" and all that the phrase brings to mind. The decorations, too, peacocks, silver and glass serving pieces, antique furnishings, are symbolic of the bygone southern plantation life. A bountiful meal such as this one is perfect for holidays and weekends when only two meals are planned for the day —the midday brunch and the early supper.

East

The East calls to mind the New England and Mid-Atlantic states. It's another area rich in history and so diverse in nature that it is impossible to categorize it as all being alike. It is an area of contrasts —the cosmopolitan nature of New York and the peaceful, rural nature of parts of Vermont and Pennsylvania. It's a manufacturing and a sea fishing area. There are many elements from which to choose for your Eastern party.

Foods of the region include seafoods, berries, maple syrup, pumpkin, puddings, cider, and cheesecake. In Maine, lobster is king, and along the eastern shore of Maryland, it's crab. In an area where seafood is a main and popular dish, it is appropriate to pattern a party after the New England clambake.

The traditional clambake is cooked in a pit on the beach. A roaring fire, built onto rocks which line the shallow pit, burns until the rocks are white hot. The ashes are raked to one side and a layer of wet seaweed tossed on top of the hot rocks. Next, potatoes in muslin bags, clams, and lobsters go on the steaming rockweed, then precooked chicken and corn in husks wrapped in foil. Another layer of seaweed goes on the food and the pit is covered with wet burlap bags or canvas held in place with sand. Cooking lasts several hours.

For an inland clambake, cook seafood separately or wrapped together in foil on the grill, or make your own pit from a large fireproof container and layer the food and wet weed in it.

Plan on plenty of conversation and singing until the food is cooked. And plan on as many as four plates per person, king-size napkins, and lots of paper cups—hot cups for clam broth and cold cups for beverage. The only decorations for a clambake are the sun, sand, and sea or your backyard patio dressed with seashells and, perhaps, piles of sand for your own private beach.

West

Immediate thoughts of the West are of the past—the Wild West, cowboys and ranches, cacti and cattle. That's still true of part of the West today, but certainly not all of it. The Southwest and West Coast are havens for artists. Fine paintings, sculptures, and jewelry originate from the West. The West is the home of miles of fruit orchards, of streams teeming with trout, of mountains that climb miles high, and of rocky ocean coasts and endless deserts.

Barbecues are popular in the Southwest and Far West and so are pinto beans, tacos, and tortillas. Other foods of the area include potatoes, fresh fruit in every form, lamb, wines, and nuts. It's a cosmopolitan blend with recipes culled from those of the settlers of the West and adapted to the foods that grow in the Western regions.

For your western-brand party, try a chuck wagon special. Plan it to be casual in all ways—in dress, in entertainment, and decorations. Set up the chuck wagon table outdoors or in the family game room. For a western atmosphere, make a table of rough board planks set on sawhorses and use bandana napkins, casual pottery or patterned paper plates, iron pots for serving dishes, and a centerpiece of cacti.

Keep your menu casual, too. The food should be substantial and saucy. Try round steak dressed up as Ranch House Round Steak* and Texas-style Beans* (pinto, of course) spooned over squares of cornbread. A tossed green salad and a beverage are all that are needed for accompaniments.

If you have the room, try your hand at square dancing or round dancing. You can buy records of square-dance music or find a local caller for the evening. Or ask a friend to bring a guitar and all of the songs of the Old West he can remember for a party of singing, storytelling, and reminiscing.

A formal beach party—that's a novel ap- →
proach to a theme of the East. Chill and pack what you can, then cook the rest on the beach. A tablecloth, wine chilling in a silver wine cooler, cocktail glasses, and silver give the event a formal air not common to picnics. Nature takes care of the decorations and the atmosphere—wind whispering through sea grasses and the tangy salt air.

*recipes on page 156.

AROUND THE WORLD

Pick a country and you've selected a party theme. Foreign decors and recipes are always intriguing for guests and challenging for the hostess. It's fun to shop for little specialties that suggest your theme country and to make centerpieces, favors, tablecloths, and napkins from what you have or can find.

India

Entertain with a dinner party Indian-style with curried lamb, rice, and spicy condiments. It's especially Indian when the non-food accessories are chosen with care. Select or make a cloth from a brightly patterned material resembling a rich tapestry. Serving dishes of brass, if you have some, help add to the exotic atmosphere. Other theme touches could include woven baskets, jewelry, travel posters, and recordings of Indian music.

Sweden

The smorgasbord, a Swedish luncheon or supper of hors d'oeuvres, hot and cold meats, smoked and pickled fish, sausages, cheeses, salads, relishes, and desserts, is the perfect theme for a buffet for a large crowd. Flavor the mood with authentic Swedish decorations. Besides placing a few of the items on your buffet and individual tables, hang tapestries, straw animals, and posters around the room and fill Swedish glassware with your floral bouquets. Import shops will carry these accessories.

Create a Viking atmosphere for your tables. For the buffet, laden a Viking ship with flowers. Card tables to seat the crowd wear two cloths—one floor length, the second, a smaller bright-bordered square. The quaint candelabra started out as a wool-winder to which have been added stubby candles and wooden gnomes nailed to the four corners. The napkin rings are yarn-wrapped paper cores with fancy matches glued on top. Hobby and craft shops carry straw figures you could use instead of the wool-winder.

← **Great condiments** for the Curried Lamb* dinner are sliced green onion, shredded coconut, whole preserved kumquats, mango chutney, golden raisins, and shelled peanuts. Heavy serving bowls with rich inlays add to the table setting and to the theme. If they're not available, use plain wooden bowls —they're just as effective.

The foods of other countries are often seasoned differently than most people are used to. So be sure to warn guests beforehand that you're planning the foreign fare.

*recipes on 156-157.

Polynesia

The luau is one of the most popular of party themes. The fresh fruit, roasted meat, and sweet-sour sauces are favorite flavors and the exotic decorations are easily obtained and emulated. Have guests sit on pillows or directly on the grass and serve the meal on long, flat boards placed on the ground and covered with cloths or imitation grass. Be sure to offer each guest a lei—either of paper or inexpensive flowers.

The Orient

The oriental theme is another popular and easy-to-plan theme. Paper decorations are inexpensive and readily available at party supply shops. Lacquerware, teapots, no-handle teacups, and serving baskets are also easily obtainable. Serve guests at low tables and give each a pair of chopsticks to use—and to take home. A simple arrangement of one or two blossoms in a bud vase is all you need for a centerpiece.

←**The exotic luau** features Kona chicken*, steamed rice, Batter-fried Shrimp*, Chinese peas with water chestnuts*, Waikiki Salad*, Raspberry sherbet with coconut, and Beach Boy Punch*. Ti leaves substitute for a tablecloth.

*recipes on pages 158-159.

At a Sukiyaki* party the hostess starts the festivities by cooking at the table while the guests sample the Chawan-Mushi* (Japanese Custard soup). The dessert is simple to prepare and serve—chilled peaches and fortune cookies.

Rich, dark colors of weathered boards and paneling lend a note of authenticity to this "medieval" setting. The roughly textured candles add, too, to the mood and provide just enough light for a pleasant dining atmosphere. Pewter serving pieces may not be available to you, but you can use dark pottery just as effectively. Your menu can carry the rest of the theme.

← **Create instant ruins** for your Greek party. Classical columns can be made from rolled-up corrugated paper, sprayed with white paint, then coated with an uneven layer of flour-and-water paste. The elegant table runners are made with notion-counter gold braid sewed in the Greek key design on white fabric remnants. Grapes and leaves complete the picture.

YESTERDAY TO TOMORROW

A variation on the "pick a country" theme is to pick a time in history, then plan your decorations and menu around that time. Visit the library for reference material and adapt the ideas you find to what is available today.

Ancient Greece

Select the glorious age of Greece when the very wealthy could throw lavish feasts for hundreds. You need not invite that many, but you can make the theme fit however many you do invite.

For decorations, build classical columns, fill goblets with grapes, entwine leaves around the centerpiece, place laurel wreaths everywhere, and use the most elaborate dishes you have.

The menu can be an adaptation or one of Greece today. Serve Moussaka*, a ground beef and eggplant casserole,

with a mixed green salad and crusty bread or rolls. For a lavish dessert or late evening snack, serve Karidopita* (a rich walnut cake), Kourabiedes* (butter cookies), Tyropitakia* (cheese pastry), fresh fruit, and strong black coffee.

Middle Ages

This is the time to serve the wild game your husband brought home last fall and winter. Venison, duck, and wild goose are the beginning of a Middle Ages party. Add a salad, wild rice and mushrooms, gravy, bread, and tankards of hot mulled cider or wine.

Improvise a medieval setting by constructing a table from weathered boards set on sawhorses. If you have pewter serving pieces available, use those and make a centerpiece from an assortment of richly colored candles.

recipes on pages 160-161.

Today

Today's young moderns can make a festive party from whatever is on hand at any time. Their ingenuity and creativity are symbols of today. To use "today" as a party theme could include all of the happy, impromptu elements of today—speedy, but elegant meals, double-duty serving pieces and furnishings, bright, gay patterns played against patterns, an informal atmosphere—it could include symbols of the happenings of the time—a spaceship orbiting the moon, miniskirts and maxi-coats, love beads and fur vests, political posters, and mock-demonstration signs.

Combine all of the "now" symbols into a pop-art wall and sit on giant pillows that resemble pop bottles and traffic signs. You can even serve your beverages in soup-can glasses for a contemporary "pop" party. For entertainment, provide the music of today and dancing.

The op art theme is another approach to a "today" party. Line the walls with optical illusion posters, make place mats from "op" wrapping paper or wallpaper, have guests dress in mod styles. For entertainment you might provide paint, masking tape, rulers, a wall covered with brown paper, and let each guest become an artist. It might be a good idea to paint in the basement or cover your rug with newspapers and plastic.

Using whatever is available for your decorations and furnishings is also a "today" theme. If serving space is limited, paint a ladder and use the rungs for the buffet serving area. Make a lively tablecloth from inexpensive fabric and match the napkins to it.

A contemporary birthday party with the "today" theme shows the ingenuity of the young hostess. Bright, happy colors set the mood in the centerpiece of packages and in the tablecloth.

The menu is an easy-to-prepare, spicy Mexican banquet—tamale pie*, chili beans, tomato chili sauce, buttered tortillas, and a green salad with onion rings, coffee, and fresh fruit.

Tomorrow

A "tomorrow" theme lets your imagination take over. What will the future be like? Imagine it, then have fun putting your tomorrow party together.

The future theme lets you try daring new recipes using convenience foods and fast-cooking methods. Experiment with the freeze-dried foods and dehydrated foods or serve make-your-own frozen dinners. There are instant foods and beverages that taste party-good and are easy and fun to prepare.

Clear plastic, glass, sparkling silver, and mirror glass make appropriate decorating elements. Set your table using an all silver color scheme, or all plastic, or all black and white. Use the disposable plastic plates and glasses or paper ones in modern patterns. You might even try making a tablecloth from vinyl, clear plastic, or paper.

There are many ways to entertain your guests or let them entertain themselves using the "tomorrow" theme. Project the future of each guest or have each one write a story of what life will be like in the 21st century. Science fiction buffs could bring a favorite book and retell the tale or read special passages aloud. To add to the merriment, ask guests to come dressed in their interpretation of the styles of the future.

If you need a reason to have a party theme in this vein, use it to celebrate a young executive's promotion, to watch a television news special on the future, or to honor the arrival of a new child and forecast its future. A future theme should be an easy and entertaining one for you to adapt to any situation.

This buffet of the future features a sparkling "tomorrow" centerpiece of glass, mirrors, and candles set on silver oilcloth. The feeling is one of space and definitely of time to come. You can construct a similar setting by gluing odd bits of mirror to tall, rectangular chunks of wood and placing them in and around a rectangular bowl. Add any types of candles you'd like (recipes on page 161).

AROUND-THE-CLOCK OCCASIONS

Any time of the day or night can be a party time—there are no limits. You can start or end your day with a festive gathering, or place it in the middle of the day. Every hostess should have in her repertoire of plans the right formulas for these parties. These plans should include the mid- or late-morning brunch, a noon luncheon, an afternoon tea and open house, an early evening supper, the versatile cocktail party, the semi-formal and formal dinners, and the late-late supper.

The time of day you choose to give your party will determine the kind of party it will be, in most cases. You will have some choice because some parties can be held at different times. From 10:00 a.m. until noon you could give a brunch or a morning coffee. At 5:00 p.m. you could have an informal supper or a cocktail party. At 8:00 p.m. the semi-formal dinner or a dessert-coffee would be equally appropriate.

The time will determine what you will serve and what are your limits.

There may be occasions when you'll need to give several parties in one or two days—when you have week-end guests or when the holiday fills your social calendar. It's essential then to know how to produce the many kinds of parties for different hours of the day, and to know which occasions are best suited to a particular time of day. Although the hectic days of entertaining morning, noon, and evening may be rare, it is necessary to know what to do when those times do arrive so that you will cope with them with ease and with confidence.

With a working knowledge of how to produce any of the time-of-day occasions, you have the foundations learned for any kind of party for any occasion. These are the essentials in your how-to-give-a-party notebook that qualify you for your superior rating as a hostess.

←**A party-time brunch** for over-night guests, for a wedding shower, or for your neighbors starts the day beautifully—especially when you serve parfaits of ice cream, strawberries, and sugar-coated corn flakes, a coffee ring made from refrigerated breakfast rolls, and Canadian-style bacon.

MID-MORNING BRUNCH

MID-MORNING BRUNCH

The brunch borrows the best from both breakfast and lunch. It's an easy form of entertaining, and it is a pleasant change from clock-watching, on-the-run weekday breakfasts. It's also the kind of meal that adapts well to late-comers and happy lingerers. Though it is an informal and hearty kind of hospitality, a brunch should still have those little extras that spell a festive gathering.

How many? This is a case of "come-one-come-all" with guests invited to bring their own guests. Numbers and the time are flexible—the only restriction being that the brunch usually takes place on weekends or holiday mornings.

The most common time for beginning a brunch is eleven o'clock, but an hour in either direction is perfectly acceptable. It is a wise idea not to set up your brunch earlier than ten in consideration of late sleepers. And if your brunch is scheduled for a Sunday morning, you might make yours an hour later for church-going guests.

A brunch can be executed overnight, to meet a sudden entertaining emergency—or organized weeks in advance. Only the amount of food to be prepared will affect the length of your planning. The brunch can feature one stellar main dish with rolls and hot beverage as simple accessories, or it can take the form of an elaborate smorgasbord.

Usually brunch menus feature a fruit or fruit juice, hot breads or toast, assorted jams and jellies, a meat or meat casserole, and eggs. Coffee, tea, or hot chocolate are standard beverages.

To give yourself more time, take advantage of warming trays and electric or insulated dishes to keep your food temptingly hot all morning long. You can prepare well in advance of guest arrivals with the assurance that food will still be at its delectable best.

The mechanics

You'll want to seat all your guests, but undoubtedly the dining room table will not be adequate. So consider using a number of bridge tables. If space is limited, all or a few of the tables can be set up at the last minute.

Folding snack trays will also be a valuable addition if you run out of card table space. But have a solid eating area and comfortable chair for each guest, even if you must use the end tables and your coffee table.

Make your tables especially inviting with card table covers, available in limitless styles and colors, or with small, decorative place mats. A centerpiece isn't necessary and sometimes space prohibits it completely. But if you have four square inches of space in the center of the table, arrange a goblet with a small boutonniere of flowers or a miniscule basket of blossoms.

Place your plates on the serving cart, flatware and napkins on a nearby buffet or at place settings on the card tables. Make things easy for the guests with individual salt and pepper and cream and sugar on each table.

A brunch is not always a last minute affair. It can be geared to such important social functions as engagement announcements, wedding breakfasts, and the celebration of a baby christening. Consider a brunch also to send sportsmen on their way, whether it's for hunting or football, and let the wives visit leisurely over the coffee. Just as much fun is the bridge brunch. Or consider a brunch as an all-family beginning for a hike in the woods or a local historical spot. An invitation by phone is all that is needed for real enjoyment, and you'll enjoy your mid-morning brunch every bit as much as your guests.

Treat your guests to a hearty English-style → breakfast right off the grill. Serve plump sausages, ham and deviled scrambled eggs*, herbed tomato slices*, butter-browned mushrooms, frosted crescent rolls, a hot fruit compote, and plenty of coffee. Keep it all at a perfect serving temperature with an electric serving cart. You'll make your friends feel like the landed gentry.

*recipes on page 162.

THE LUNCHEON

The midday lunch is a popular event for committee meetings, business conclaves, bridge parties, and social chatter gatherings. In the pleasant atmosphere of a noonday party, often more is accomplished than at meetings held during any other hour of the day.

The luncheon can take a multitude of forms—a substantial men-invited lunch; the light, ladies-only lunch; the dessert luncheon; the buffet luncheon; bridge luncheon, and fund-raising bazaar or style-show lunch.

With the exception of the dessert luncheon, the general arrangements for a noontime party are the same as for an evening dinner. You'll invite guests, plan the menu, decorate the table and room, plan your space arrangements, and set up a time schedule.

You will, however, probably want to plan a lighter meal than you would for a dinner. Two or three courses are sufficient. If men are invited, make the courses hardy. If it's women only, the menu can be simpler, dainty, and even a bit fancy. In most every group there are a few who are diet-conscious. They will appreciate the non-gooey foods such as fresh fruit and light salads.

Cocktails before a luncheon are optional. If you do serve before-luncheon drinks, be sure to have some light beverages and some nonalcoholic ones. Serve the drinks and a light assortment of canapes in the living or family room.

Invitations

A phone call or personal invitation is all that's really necessary for an informal gathering of good friends. If the group is larger and it is meeting for business reasons, or if it is to be a bridge gathering for several tables, then send informal notes at least a week before the luncheon. If the luncheon is a regularly scheduled meeting, your club's secretary will probably call to remind members of the event. But if it is a semiformal luncheon, written invitations are required in the same form as those sent for a dinner party. Mail them out about two weeks before the party.

Even if your luncheon is casual enough for in-person invitations, be sure your guests have all of the time, place, and date information correctly.

Setting up

Cheerful colors, flowers, and a pretty table arrangement can set the mood for your luncheon. Iron your liveliest or most sophisticated colored linen table cloth or pull out your prettiest place mats, then coordinate your centerpiece (minus candles). It's just as important to have your dishes and flatware sparkling clean at lunch as for an evening dinner. And keep the table uncluttered for an unspoiled effect.

Prepare the table and the food as much as possible in advance. You can set your food out buffet style. This is sometimes preferred to a table setting. But this applies generally to women. They are more at ease balancing a plate on their laps than are men. Or, set everything on a sideboard close to you and serve a family style luncheon.

To simplify picking-up at a bridge luncheon, serve the meal at the dining table and reserve the bridge tables for bridge. If you haven't enough space at your table, cover the bridge tables with pretty removable cloths.

The versatile luncheon is a perfect occasion for introducing new acquaintances to friends, for honoring a special guest (a new neighbor, perhaps), to organize a charity bazaar, or just to chat with close friends.

Luncheon meetings can accomplish near-→ miracles and be bright and colorful, too. For this craft-bazaar luncheon the menu is a hearty autumn fare. Lobster-Shrimp Chowder* is easy to make from frozen soups and seafood. Serve crackers, crusty rolls, cherry tomatoes, olives, and celery with the chowder. Add Pineapple Delight Cake* and freshly brewed coffee to complete the menu.

*recipes on page 162.

THE AFTERNOON TEA

The tea is one of the most traditional and feminine forms of entertaining. It's a perfect way to gather friends for a pleasant afternoon, to introduce someone special (a new daughter-in-law, perhaps), to honor an out-of-town distinguished guest, to close an important social organization meeting, or just to chat with favorite acquaintances.

The time for a tea is socially prescribed. It falls in the afternoon between the hours of three and six. The time is stated definitely on the invitation, a calling card or fold-over note card, "from three-thirty until five" or "from four until five-thirty." Do mail the invitations about two weeks before the tea.

The nature of the tea makes it adaptable to all age groups. Invite your friends of all ages and all interests. The formality of the tea is a common bond among guests and the conversation will flow smoothly and constantly.

The number of people you invite is also flexible. A tea is perfect for a large guest list since the crowd will be mobile all during the prescribed hours and preparations are at a minimum.

It is also a perfect occasion for intimate conversation with a few close friends. You can save it to announce something very special, such as an engagement or a coming baby.

The large tea

Preparations for the large tea will take a bit more time than for the smaller, intimate tea. Begin by selecting the site —you'll need a large table and room enough for people to move along it freely. Pick your prettiest linen or lace tablecloth, unless the wood finish on your table is one you'd like to show off. If you don't have a dining table large enough to hold everything easily, put two smaller tables together, cover the gap, then use a floor length cloth. See that your silver is at its shiniest and your china sparkling. Set a centerpiece of flowers and candles.

Choose the party fare with a variety of both color and flavor in mind. Blend colors freely; use both light and dark breads. Alternate tasty, sweet and non-sweet fillings on your petite sandwiches. You can make the sandwiches the morning of the tea, wrap well in plastic or waxed paper, and store in the refrigerator. Mints, bonbons, and nuts will add to the attractiveness of your table.

Tradition styles the setting of the tea table. The tea service and its accompaniments, sugar and creamer, small salver of lemons daintily sliced or wedged, small serving fork, sugar tongs, tea strainer, and, optionally, a slop bowl, sit at one end of the table. The punch or coffee service is at the other end. Cups and saucers are placed at the left of the service trays, teaspoons and napkins at the right. The sandwiches, cakes, cookies, nuts, mints, and small plates are set in easy reach along the side of the table.

When the tea is a large one, ask friends to help pour. It's a good idea to have two or three friends ready to relieve the others after each hour of serving. You'll also need someone in the kitchen preparing trays and checking the hot water supply.

The small tea

The small tea can take various forms. If it's for a very few, serve it in the living room using the coffee table or other low serving table. The hostess pours and serves only cold sandwiches or cookies, unless she has kitchen help and can manage a few warm items.

At another small tea, the hostess may prepare nonperishable cookies and have the makings for sandwiches available for guests to make their own.

Of course, at any tea, the tea itself must be the best. Choose a tested tea that's not too pungent nor too spicy. Make it properly, then watch the atmosphere glow with the warmth of the freshly brewed tea.

Christmastime is a perfect time to gather a group of your favorite friends for an afternoon tea. Serve trays of your yuletide sweets and sandwiches and a holly-green punch to complement the season and the freshly brewed tea. Tea table decorations, always elegant and feminine, have their theme built in with the festive season. Topiary trees studded with holly and blue ribbon bows and a cascading ivy waterfall grace this setting.

Our holiday menu calls for a few things sweet and a few things not, a few dark colors and a few light—all served on the best and shiniest of silver trays. Contrasts in color, taste, and texture add to eating pleasure as well as to the beauty of the tea table. Pictured here are Tuna Rounds*, Nut Bread Sandwiches*, Sugar Cookies*, Thumbprints*, Lemon Tea Cakes*, nuts and mints, Lime Frosted Punch*, and, of course, the tea.

OPEN HOUSE

The Open House—a marvelous way to entertain from 20 to 100 in one afternoon. You'll have a chance to visit with many friends and perhaps to meet your husband's business associates or the spouses of your bridge club members. It will be enjoyable and easy to handle provided you have a plan.

Plan first the number of people to invite. This will depend on the size of your home and how many you can prepare for. If you invite over 20 or 25, stagger the hours of the party. Divide your list into two or three groups and invite the first group from one to three, the second from two to four, and the third from three to five (holiday or weekend afternoons are best). This will keep the number of guests in your home at one time within comfortable limits and allow you to handle a large guest list.

To invite your guests, send hand-written notes. Then every recipient will have a visible reminder of the time, address, and date. If you should phone the invitations, ask your guests to jot the information down.

Almost anything can be served at an open house, but you still require a plan. Some hostesses prefer a menu that gives a full meal in an afternoon of bite-size proportions. A typical example is the one pictured opposite with ham, dips, fruit, and sweets. Or your menu might include trays of your specially concocted hors d'oeuvres. To be on the safe side, augment your exotic delicacies with some favorite standbys such as assortments of crackers, cheeses, and dips.

Do all of the food preparation in advance of the party. During the festivities, you might have someone in the kitchen arranging hors d'oeuvres on plates. Recruit your own teen-age daughter or hire a schoolgirl. This frees you to keep your eye on the table and to make a quick trip to the kitchen when something needs replenishing.

Assign the beverage department to the host, or, if constant beverage service is required for guests, hire someone for the job so the host will be free to circulate among the guests. It is perfectly acceptable to serve guests their first beverage and to suggest that they help themselves to any refills.

Plan early where to set up the serving table—one end of the living room is a logical spot. Your table should be out of the general flow of traffic, but it should be easy to reach. If possible, set your table out from the wall so that guests can circulate around it. A separate table can be set up for beverages. If the dining room is adjacent to the living room, easily accessible, and big enough for a buffet, by all means put the dining table to use.

What about seating arrangements? Your usual furniture arrangement will be perfectly adequate since few guests sit at this type of party.

As everyone will be roaming from group to group, you should, too. It's your job as hostess to introduce people, get conversations started, and see that everyone is enjoying himself.

For the physical comfort of your guests, keep the heat down, trafficways open, and ventilation good. See that ashtrays are accessible and emptied often. Your guests will appreciate the attention and consideration—both smokers and non-smokers.

When guests first start arriving, have soft, instrumental background music playing. When the number of guests increases and conversation picks up, inconspicuously turn the music off. As the guests thin out, quietly fade the music in again. It's all a part of your master plan—and that plan can guarantee your hostessing success.

◄—**Very special hors d'oeuvres** help make a very special open house, and these don't require hours to fix. Surprise guests with Irish coffee and Cappuccino and a tray of sweets. This easy-do menu calls for guacamole dip, chutney-cheddar spread, caviar on cream cheese, thin-sliced ham on mustard-rye rounds, coconut meringues,* tassies,* tri-level brownies,* Irish coffee,* and Cappuccino.*

recipes on pages 164-165.

INFORMAL SUPPER PARTIES

Potluck suppers and teen gatherings have the reputation for being carefree, relaxing, and thoroughly fun for everyone—even the hostess. But, like every other kind of party, it's the detail work that can make the party click.

The Potluck Party

Potlucks are just right for neighborhood or relative gatherings. If your potluck is going to include several families, check to see whether someone might be having house guests and invite them, too. The potluck has this advantage— it's so flexible you can easily enlarge your guest capacity.

Next, determine how you want to make the invitations—you can phone or send hand-written notes if you wish. But if you should phone invitations, be sure to follow with a note reminding the guests what they are to bring.

Get the invitations out at least ten days before the party. This gives each cooking guest time to plan her dish and make that important trip to the store.

The question often arises in planning potluck dinners—should the hostess plan the menu and assign dishes to each of her guests or should she let each guest bring her specialty? Probably the easiest way is to suggest categories (meat dishes, vegetable dishes, salads, desserts) and let each guest bring her favorite in her category. But the hostess should provide all of the condiments, rolls, and beverages.

The day before the party, call each guest to ask what dish she's bringing and whether it will be hot or cold.

If your potluck is going to be an outdoor-summer affair and guests will bring refrigerated dishes, plan to have several beds of crushed ice at the buffet table. In addition, there are new cold servers to keep food chilled, or you might use the family ice chest, or a small camping refrigerator.

To keep hot dishes hot, run a heavy-duty extension cord with several outlets to the buffet table. Then you might suggest bringing the food in the electric skillet or saucepan in which it was prepared. An electric warming tray is ideal if you happen to have one.

Seating the Entourage

Finding enough seats is often a problem for any hostess. Very few homes can seat 20 to 25 people without extra provisions. A convenient solution is to rely on your local rental service.

For a summer lawn party, rent folding tables. They're generally available in six- and eight-foot lengths, and prices average $2.00 per table for 24 hours.

If your potluck is going to be a winter-indoors affair and you have enough floor space available, ask each family to bring a card table to the party. Whether you use card tables or long family-styled tables, plan to rent folding chairs to make sure each guest has adequate seating during the meal. Chairs, too, are available at about 20 cents apiece if you're renting 25 or less, or 15 cents each for more than 25. (Prices can vary in different areas.)

While you're making arrangements for table space, don't overlook the extra table you'll want to set for your buffet service. Depending on the number of guests and the number of dishes to be served, you may want more than one table. Allow plenty of room for guests to serve themselves easily.

For tableware, paper plates are the answer. Many attractive patterns are available to let you set a good-looking buffet table and still take most of the work out of post-party cleanup.

When you're contracting your rental service, you may want to rent flatware, too. Prices are reasonable, usually 35 to 40 cents per dozen pieces. And during peak entertaining seasons, around holidays and during summer months, plan to call your rental service and reserve your items at least one week in advance of your supper party.

Young People's Party

Teen-agers enjoy hosting their own affairs, and tend to the informal. The two essentials are music and plenty of food —but this is still a good time for them to learn the graces of entertaining.

Invitations should be sent out and should be very specific about the date, place, and time, including an estimated departure time. Parents, too, should be well informed of the party time and place arrangements.

One good rule—keep an adult at hand, but in the background. Teens don't want to feel supervised, whether they need it or not.

Spicy, hot, unusual foods seem to be teen favorites. Be sure also to have a good supply of soft drinks and nibbling items of all kinds at easy reach.

Set your food buffet-style. Teen-agers would rather roam from chair to chair, or from group to group, even while eating, than be confined to a table.

Do not make costly table settings. Paper plates or plastic tableware are much easier on your budget. Young people are more interested in having a good time than in your good pottery or china. And if accidents do happen, the damage will be minimal.

This is your teen-ager's party, so make him or her partly responsible for its success. Let the youngster plan his own party and send the invitations. If your teen-age daughter is giving the party, she should help with the food preparation. And either a son or daughter should be completely in charge of the cleanup duties. Be sure your teen understands his duties before the party starts. This kind of party is not only good fun, but good training for the time when your teen-ager becomes a full-fledged host or hostess.

The Teen-age party—easy-to-serve and easy-to-eat foods are teen favorites. They'll devour these Tamale Hero Sandwiches*, hot from the oven, with their tempting aroma of chili and melting cheddar cheese. Plate partners of corn chips and "pickle-sickles" are designed for easy eating. Make the ice cream cones and cookies ahead of time—a good project for your young party-giver to do.

SUPPER PARTIES

Suppers, not as informal as a potluck nor as formal as a dinner, used to be strictly family affairs. Now they have become casual, informal meals abounding with good food and friends. Traditional suppers were served at six, but today, depending on the evening's plans, you can serve it at any time in half an hour. All you need is the makings of a beef fondue and some salad greens.

A fast and fun fondue party is the perfect solution for last-minute entertaining. You can send up the flare by a quick phone call the day of your supper or you can invite guests by note only one or two days in advance.

How to give a supper party

In this case, protocol doesn't demand written invitations and most hostesses find a call much easier and more convenient. However, written invitations can be your own novel inventions, such as, sending a fork with the message "to be filled at the Dunnes, 407—98th Street, Friday the 17th at 7."

Often supper parties precede or follow some gala event—a concert, a movie-premiere, or little or big theater. And despite the supper party's easy, casual air—it should have an aura of elegance. Flowers and greens are a nice addition. Make sure cigarette boxes are full and lighters are working.

A supper party can appear to be delightfully spontaneous, but it does require some preparation during the day, if you want to enjoy the evening and still be a gracious, cool, and competent hostess. If the supper is to be before the event, you'll need to have precise time plans so you all arrive at the theater or concert at the right hour. Plan a menu of easy-to-eat foods that can be placed on a buffet or table and kept warm. The fondue, tossed green salad, and crusty French bread idea would fit a hurried schedule perfectly.

Your food should be prepared the afternoon of the party. Have a plastic bag of salad greens chilled and ready in the refrigerator. If you're serving a meat fondue, the meat should be cubed and refrigerated. Then all that is left to do is place the cooking dishes on the table, set out the plate and forks, and heat the cooking oil. From there on, guests take over to cook their own.

The number of guests you invite is up to you. You can invite more than you would to a sit-down dinner, for chairs are no problem. The floor or floor pillows can easily serve as seats. And you don't have to bother with individual serving trays or elaborate table space for each guest. Most people prefer the coffee table in the living room as the focal point of the party.

If you're serving fondue and inviting 15 or more, you'll want to prepare two fondue centers because only five or six people can comfortably cook in the same area. Try placing the salad and beverages on a different table or in another room to keep the group mobile.

Supper party entertainment

Good conversation is the order of the evening. Most everyone will have opinions to express, so music, even the unobtrusive background kind, is far from necessary. Games of all kinds are good additions to this type of animated and freewheeling party. But pick games meant for a large group of people so everyone can get into the act. And choose relaxing, enjoyable games. Often, late night hours are not the time for mentally strenuous contests. But anytime is the right time for friendly, relaxed supper party at your house.

Elegant beef fondue * gives each guest an active → role in your party. Each person spears a cube of beef tenderloin with a fondue fork, holds it in bubbling cooking oil till it's done. Then, after transferring the meat to a plate and cool dinner fork, it's dipped into any of a variety of well-seasoned butters and sauces. Have crusty rolls, a green salad, and cake for go-alongs.

*recipes on page 165.

THE DINNER PARTY

Though putting on a dinner party requires a high degree of preparation, the rewards are many and not easily forgotten. The goal of every hostess is twofold: Have the guests enjoy the cuisine, and relish in the warmth of companionship and shared interests. It's not difficult to accomplish if you follow a day-by-day blueprint for a dinner party (semiformal in this case. The truly formal dinner requires finger bowls and doilies, kitchen help, and waiters).

Begin with the guest list. The formal dinner once required a list ranging from 12 to 24. But smaller numbers and smaller tables (the average dining table with leaves added does not seat more than eight comfortably) are more manageable, and better geared to today's pace, especially if you're without help.

Don't be afraid of odd numbers. Feel free to ask the summer bachelor or the piano teacher you would like to know better. Five or seven are no more trouble to entertain than six or eight.

For this event, give the guests a week to ten days advance notice. A small note is still the best invitation. Clearly state the time, place, and date; include an RSVP, and, state formal or semiformal dress. Your invitations should be handwritten in ink on your personal informals, monogrammed, or initialed note paper, or simple notes.

Dinner at eight used to be the approved time, but even firm rules of etiquette are subject to change. Many couples prefer a later time—perhaps eight-thirty or nine.

At least three days before the party take a detailed inventory of your table settings. This is the time to press the creases from the tablecloth, fold napkins, polish flatware and hollow ware, decide on the flowers you'll be ordering or cutting from the garden, and, of course, plan the menu.

Do any strenuous housecleaning at least two days ahead of time. Early in the morning of the party day, set the table completely (see table setting diagram on page 122) and arrange the centerpiece. If you're alarmed about dust, cover the table with tissue paper or plastic dry cleaning bags.

The centerpiece requires candles as well as flowers. Any back-of-the-table arrangement can be luxuriantly full; but for the center of the table, flowers should not exceed 14 inches in height.

What and how to serve

The foods you serve can make the difference between enjoying your own party and working yourself to a frazzle. Foods you can prepare ahead, at least partially, are your best bet. Your main course should be centered around oven-prepared meat. Let your oven cook it then hold it warm for serving. Prepare first course or salads in the afternoon and refrigerate.

You can set a formal dinner table and place the food on the buffet for guests to help themselves if you wish. Or you can use what is sometimes referred to as "New England service" with a light first course on a plate on top of the dinner plate and the food ready to be served lined up before the host. First course plates are quickly removed to an adjacent cart or tray and the feast is then dispensed by the host. After the main course, dinner plates are whisked away to the waiting cart and coffee and dessert brought over by the hostess from a nearby table or buffet.

Music is a must, but make it the soft kind, a happy muted background for the hum of conversation which means that your special evening has been a well-planned and beautiful success.

You can roast this handsome brace of ducks, to → serve with a flavorful cranberry sauce, in about two hours. The rest is planned around do-aheads. The menu: Pineapple Shrub*, assorted crackers, Brace of Ducklings*, Wild Rice Casserole*, Frenched green beans, spiced peaches and crabapples, Bibb lettuce salad, Curry Dressing*, rolls, butter, Mincemeat Ice Cream Tarts*, demitasse.

*recipes on page 166.

THE COCKTAIL PARTY

The cocktail party can be whatever you want it to be. It can be the largest party you can arrange or an intimate gathering of eight. It can last a designated two hours or be an indefinite come-when-you-can and stay-for-dinner plan with no time limit. You can serve simple dips, spreads, and crackers, a variety of hot and cold canapes, or an entire buffet meal. Each has its advantages.

Perhaps the happy, noisy chatter and the informality of the large crush makes the cocktail a popular form of party. There is a companionship in a large crowd with everyone standing, then moving from group to group, and nibbling on the bite-size tidbits. Even though it is informal, both the large and small cocktail party require advance planning.

Decide first on the size. You can invite and invite without worrying about chairs because few will sit. If, however the party is a prelude to another event—a dinner dance or a movie, you may want to restrict the number so that everyone will get off in time and you won't be hampered by lingerers.

Invitations can be in any form. You can telephone them, write them on note cards or visiting cards, or send pre-printed ones you fill in. Usually you state a definite time span sometime between the hours of 5:00 and 9:00 p.m. Add an R.s.v.p. if you wish—it's not necessary, but you may want to have some idea of how much food to prepare.

What you can serve at a cocktail party is almost limitless. The general rule is that no matter what you serve, every-thing be in bite-size proportions and be finger foods. You can serve small bits of meat, cheese, vegetables, and fruit on wooden picks, tiny open-faced sand-wiches, seafood bites and sauces, tiny stuffed pastries, dips, dunks, spreads, and crackers. Some can be served hot and some cold. If you are planning to hold the party sans help, limit yourself to about four types of foods (be sure to plan a variety) and only one hot dish—unless you have hot trays and flame-heated casseroles to keep hot food hot. If you try to do too much you'll be spending your entire time in the kitchen.

For beverages plan on at least three types of liquors. The minimum would be gin or vodka, Scotch, and bourbon. You can add others (rum, blends) if you like. Be sure to have mixes (the instant kind are especially handy), soft drinks, and a punch or eggnog for those who don't like cocktails. Vermouth, lime juice, and lemon juice are nice additions and are necessary for many drinks.

Hostess duties begin, of course, with the invitations and food preparation. Then be sure you have plenty of glasses, napkins and coasters, and big ashtrays and that the bartender has ample bar equipment. Arrange the house so that people can move freely around the room, the bar, and the snack tables. If it's a really large party, you might consider setting up two bars with one at each end of the room—a table covered with a waterproof cloth will do for a bar. If it's a small gathering, the kitchen counter can be the bar.

When you're doing the party alone, you'll welcome guests and pass the snacks around and the host will tend the bar. It is proper to stop taking the snack trays around and place them on a table when the party is well under way. If you do have help, the helpers can tend bar, and pass drinks and snacks to the guests during the entire evening.

For guests' comfort, be sure that the ventilation is good, ashtrays accessible and emptied often, trafficways cleared of tippy furniture, and snacks within everyone's easy reach.

Background music should be handled as for an open house. It's nice at first when guests are arriving. When the hum of conversation increases, switch the music off, then bring it back again as the party begins to break up.

You'll find a cocktail party for a large number of people easier to prepare and give than it appears and everyone will enjoy it as much as you do.

recipes appear on page 167.

Any size group would enjoy a combination of hot and cold appetizers—seafood, ground beef, and cheese. It's a good variety and looks as taste-tempting as it really is. Serve the hot duo-Peppy Beef Dip* and broiled, bacon-wrapped shrimp* in a keep-warm server. Serve crackers with the Edam-Sage spread*. Hollow out an Edam cheese, mix the cheese with spices and sour cream, and return it to the shell. Hot Cranberry Glogg* is an ideal go-along.

Pass an Antipasto tray* for a gourmet flair. Vegetables, eggs, tuna, and cheese are popular party fare and can be served on crackers, or alone. They offer the variety in color and flavor necessary for a pretty party table.

In the bowl at the left: Fresh Relish Italiano and Avocado Cuts with Salami. Center: Olive-stuffed Eggs, sharp cheese. Right: Marinated Artichoke Hearts and Tonno al Limone. Serve small chunks of French bread and crackers.

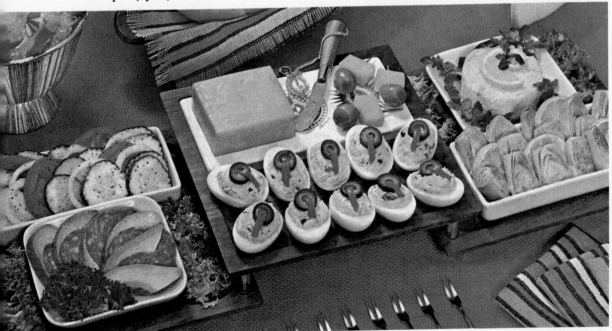

LATE-NIGHT SUPPERS

Late-night occasions call for special entertaining and the little, late supper is making the scene. Whether it's après ski or after-the-show, the midnight supper is a perfect time to discuss the night's events with special friends in a cozy, congenial atmosphere.

The late supper can be as spontaneous as saying, "come to our house after the concert" or as carefully planned as a semiformal dinner. Your invitations can be both spontaneous and planned. Invite some before with notes, include a few more during the evening.

Let seating and table space be your guide to generosity in determining how many extras to invite since this is likely to be a sit-down meal.

If you're planning on a large number of guests for a sit-down dinner (10-18), you might try a seated buffet. Set up tables for four or six (card tables or round plywood disks on card tables) covered with floor-length cloths, and use your dining table or sideboard top for setting up the buffet service.

The seated buffet is informal, but still elegant enough for a late-hour supper. Each guest has a chair and a place to sit and does not have to balance a plate on his knee in a corner of the room. The food can be more elegant than a stand-up buffet dinner also, since you would not need to worry about finger-foods vs. fork-foods.

The meal served at this late hour should be light, but substantial, easy to fix, and easy to serve. Guests may not have eaten for several hours, but probably did eat a supper or dinner before the evening's festivities. A two or three course meal of a chowder or a quiche, a salad, and dessert should be plenty for this late evening hour.

The most important thing about what you serve is the time it takes to prepare it. Above all else, choose something that can be put together ahead of time and heated at the last minute. Plan to have the food ready to serve within minutes after your guests arrive.

*recipes on page 168.

Planning the supper

You'll start planning for the party as soon as the thought first enters your mind. Plan the number, or approximate number of guests, whether it's to be a sit-down buffet or an informal dinner, then call or write your invitations. Plan the menu next, remembering to allow for last-minute guest invitations.

It would be easiest for you to set the plates, serving dishes, and utensils on the buffet table and the silver, napkins, glasses, and centerpiece on the card tables before leaving for the evening. You can add another table when you get home if you've invited more.

Try to concentrate all of tables in one area of the room. Guests seated in a far corner away from the others might feel slighted and unwelcome.

Serving the supper

The easiest method of serving for the hostess who must do all of the work alone, is to have the guests help themselves to the first course and to refills. The host can be responsible for pouring the beverages, and the hostess for serving the dessert. A little more elegant way is for the guests to serve themselves the first time and for the hostess or her helper to take around the rolls, condiments, and seconds.

Good conversation is the only form of entertainment you'll need at this party. If you invite with care, selecting people with different interests, the conversation will be stimulating. Let your guests relax and savor the day, the company, and the good food.

Springtime brightness makes a late-night sup- → per fresh and appealing. This elegant meal features Shrimp Quiche* (you can do most of it ahead) in individual pastry shells. Swiss and Gruyere cheeses complement the shrimp. Add Hearts of Palm Salad* with tangy dressing, crisp bread sticks, Fresh Rhubarb Cup*, and Sugar-Pecan Crisps* to complete the special occasion menu.

SPECIAL OCCASION PARTIES

From infancy to gracious maturity there are special events in everyone's life. There may be once-in-a-lifetime occasions or they may be annual occurrences, but they all have a personal importance and warrant some form of recognition.

The earliest special occasion and the one that is observed most often is the birthday. For the youngsters the parties are often elaborate with cake, ice cream, party games, and festive decorations a must. With the exception of the landmark birthdays—sixteen, twenty-one, and fifty —the late-teen and adult years are celebrated quietly and only with close friends and family. Occasionally an adult birthday is an excuse for a little more elaborate party, but the guests aren't asked to bring gifts and if they are, the cost is limited by the hostess.

Anniversaries, too, are celebrated annually and in the same ways as birthdays. If it's a particularly special one, a twenty-fifth or fiftieth, the couple is honored with an open house. The others call for smaller, more intimate affairs.

Once-in-a-lifetime occasions include graduations, weddings and pre-wedding festivities, usually housewarmings, and bon voyage parties. The latter two, however, may occur more frequently in today's moving world. These too, are an excuse for entertaining.

One of the nicest things about entertaining for special occasions is that you generally have complete liberty to give the kind of party you do and like best—for any kind can be made appropriate from women-only teas to the formal dinner-dance.

There are parties to fit any and all of the special occasions and, hopefully, you'll find just the right one in this chapter, or even in any of the other chapters, to fit the next special event for which you'll be called upon to entertain.

←**Are you honoring someone's birthday?** Maybe it's an anniversary or a friend's housewarming. Treat your guests to your own special "Ice-cream Party" held on a sunny afternoon. The main attraction will be the homemade ice cream and the variety of toppings you offer as go-alongs.

BIRTHDAYS FOR ADULTS

Birthdays are for adults, too. It's flattering to be remembered even if it is with a simple card or a verbal wish. But on this personal, very special occasion, it is especially pleasing to be honored with a birthday party.

A dinner party with the family or with a few close friends is the party answer for those birthday celebrants who prefer a quiet, pleasant celebration to a crowded gathering. Treat your honored guest to what he or she really likes. Set your prettiest table. And find out his or her favorite dishes. Ask your friend's spouse if you are not sure. This is all done to make the birthday guest feel special on his day.

For entertainment at an at-home dinner plan to show a rented movie or some very short home movies featuring the guest of honor. Horoscope reading is also an appropriate birthday pastime and every guest will enjoy hearing what is "in the stars" for him.

Decorations can be as varied as the person's interests. Plan a theme around his favorite pastime—playing cards, reading, hiking, bowling. For a woman the theme can be a bit more genteel—perhaps birthstones or flowers.

Another pleasant way to celebrate with a small guest list is a dinner at a particularly good restaurant. Then invite everyone to your home afterwards for the traditional cake and coffee.

There are particular birthdays that have special meaning—the twenty-first, the fiftieth, and any after seventy. These deserve elegant treatment.

The twenty-first birthday is the traditional entrance to legal adulthood. You could make the party a legal decree of your honoree's new step. Present him with a legal-appearing document declaring his adulthood, then present the cake and coffee—or champagne. A young adult may not want too much of a fuss, and may have plans of his own, so a simple, short gathering might be best.

The fiftieth birthday is another milestone. This might be the time to honor the celebrant with a surprise party. Plan with that person an after-dinner coffee or a buffet for one or two close friends, then invite the rest to show up just in time for the celebration. All your honoree will know is that the few are coming. Bring out the extra desserts you had hidden or the extra casseroles you had baked for the buffet and toast your guest with birthday wishes. Put on some record favorites of yesterday, bring out the yearbooks, and spend the evening spin-

MENU

Roast Rock Cornish Game Hens*

Wild Rice   Creamed Mushrooms

Buttered Broccoli Spears

Greengage Plum Salad*

Butterhorn Rolls   Butter

Burnt-sugar Cake*   *Ice Cream*

ning anecdotes of "the good old days."

To honor someone who is seventy or older, arrange a small gathering of good friends and family. A simple menu and a short time of good conversation, card games, or whatever the honored guest likes will make an enjoyable celebration. Or, if the person still enjoys a lively party, plan a reception. You might use a lavender-and-old-lace theme. Set the table in lavender and lace and decorate small cakes with lavender icing. Midafternoon or early evening is a good time for this birthday party.

Flowers and presents set this table apart as one → for a special occasion. The giant mums replace bows on the packages to continue the theme set by the end-of-the-table bouquet. Little touches like these make the birthday person feel special and make even a family meal seem like a party. A setting of large flowers like these is appropriate for a man too, as well as a woman.

Treasure-trove party: The treasure hunt is the main event of this party. Hide the key to a gaily decorated and padlocked box filled with prizes for everyone. Organize teams for the treasure search.

Hickory, Dickory, Dock: The very young will enjoy a nursery rhyme gathering. Cut a clock from a shoe box, make a paper plate face, and hang a pendulum inside. Invent "mouse" games to play.

CHILDREN'S BIRTHDAY PARTIES

Children love parties and you can probably count on a minimum of a decade of birthday parties. Since you're faced with the prospect of being chief hostess, why not consider the best possible ways to arrange the party?

Once you've been bewitched into saying "yes," you'll have to begin the invitations. Children love receiving their own mail, so do select mailable invitations. Consider the assembly-line pre-created invitations which you and your youngster can decorate—it saves starting from scratch, but provides the child with a sense of accomplishment.

How many to invite? The same number as the age of the child is a good maxim to follow up to the age of six. After this, children start asking to invite the whole class. If that is the case, offer to take cake and ice cream to the school (after consulting the teacher). For at-home parties, try to keep the number to a workable eight or ten. For the really young—up to age 7 or 8—invite those children who are your child's friends, and who are near the same age.

A good time for a party is afternoon on Saturday or weekdays for pre-schoolers or on Saturday morning or afternoon or immediately after school for six and older. It's also a good idea to keep the party short—one to two hours.

Offer to pick up all the birthday party guests and take them home again. In this way you'll gain a very important advantage. You can control the length of the party from start to end.

For help, call on another mother, a friend, or a relative. Well-supplied with helpful hands, you can now proceed with the party entertainment.

Until children are seven or eight, they won't care for organized games. Let little ones play with toys or outdoor play equipment. They might listen to a short story told by an experienced story teller just before refreshment time.

For the older children games are the first order of the day. Provide some high for removing overshoes and snowsuits and have clothespins on hand to keep mittens in pairs. If the children arrive with damp clothes or come in damp from outdoor snow games, toss the wet garments in a set-on-warm dryer.

Little touches will produce the atmosphere of a full-scale party. It's a good idea to have a little stockpile of items such as balloons, a ready-made centerpiece or two, colorful napkins, and hard candy. Then you're ready for a party anytime, without having to go to a store in inclement weather. Dress up your house for the festivities by tying balloons to chairs or lamps.

Start the party off with a couple of games but keep a wary eye out for the onset of boredom. This is your signal to send everyone outdoors before they get too actively restless. Bad weather may be an annoyance to adults, but to bundled-up children it's a challenge.

When you suggest the backyard outing, have a definite plan in mind. A good layer of snow offers tremendous creative potential. You can suggest building tunnels, arches, or igloos. Or

offer a prize for the most ima[ginative] snow sculpture. Brush up on t[he] rules of such games as "King [of the] Mountain" and "Fox and Geese" [and] be prepared to arbitrate any dif[ference] of opinion. Establish the fact t[hat you] are the only umpire.

Even gloomy, cold, snowless [days] fer possibilities for outdoor a[ction.] Suggest a relay race, a tug of [war,] a potato race with prizes awarde[d when] the children return indoors. Y[ou may] want to have a backyard scaveng[er hunt] —even if you have to plant som[e items] in advance. If you're worried abo[ut over-] exposure, set your kitchen ti[mer for] twenty or thirty minutes, then [round] up the group when the bell sound[s.]

About this time the guests [may] settle down to a quiet time and [a light] supper. You'll find soup and san[dwiches] ample fare. But don't neglect t[o top] off with ice cream or cake or bo[th. This] gives the whole affair the really [authen-] tic party note. Be sure to reserve [about] twenty minutes to gather up belo[ngings.] You'll make your homecoming d[uties easy] and guests will have happy me[mories.]

A basket of balloons simulates ice cream cones. Inflate the balloons a small fraction, tie, and run string through cones. Insert cones and artificial flowers into plastic-foam-filled basket.

"Wejams"—three of them, sprout g[reenery] and good wishes. They're from a vari[ety shop.] Wigs of air-plant (no water needed) [can be] added. Center creature is elevated on a [stand.]

Shipwreck party: Have guests come in ragged jeans and sneakers and give a prize for the most threadbare costume. A python twined around a crepe-paper tree provides the centerpiece.

Oriental Doll party: Plan a party just for little girls. Have each guest bring a doll and provide the material scraps or paper for each to make a costume. Make stilt-house homes for favors.

spot for the entertainment. It can be a rented cartoon movie—an old documentary—or a guitarist from the local high school, or some youngsters who have a knack with a puppet show. Themes at parties for older children can provide entertainment ideas, too. At a Cowboy party play western music and try a simple square dance. Or at an Outer Space theme party have commercial space games for the youngsters to play and make a rocket from cardboard.

A trip is a good party idea. Children love them and they are easy for Mother. Arrange a short excursion, with plenty of helping hands, to the zoo or a movie. Then provide the food either at an ice cream stand or at home and take the guests to their homes.

Clashes are common at parties with the very young. The best way to beat a problem is to avoid having it arise. Remove bric-a-brac and any other fragile object to a place of safety—preferably an inaccessible top shelf or a locked closet. It is wise, too, to seal or empty the medicine cabinet.

During the critical presentation of the birthday presents, offer the young

guests a small favor in exchange for the gift. They will part with the present much more willingly and you won't have a tug-of-war to contend with.

To hold prizes, favors, jelly beans, and party hats, have a good supply of grocery bags with crumpled edges, and in large letters emblazon the name of each guest on the front.

A rule-of-thumb of what to serve is— keep it simple and familiar and don't make children wait too long. You might even start the party with refreshments. If you're serving a meal, serve it at the accustomed time. Hamburgers, hot dogs, chips, and perhaps celery nibbles are still the accepted fare. Or you can serve just the traditional cake and ice cream. But be sure to have a birthday cake. To a child, a decorated cake with candles is the symbol of a birthday.

To provide a proper grace-note and to be sure all the guests depart happy, keep two baskets handy at the door. One might be filled with wrapped candy, the other with noisemakers. Shovel a generous handful of candy and a horn into the waiting decorated bag and begin your home-bound trips.

MIDWINTER PARTIES

SHOWERS/ANNIVERSARIES

Children are small, gregarious creatures. And just because there has been a heavy snowfall, streets are covered with ice, and a north wind is raging, they see no reason for being kept apart. Since a solitary child is often lonely it makes midwinter gatherings for tots nearly mandatory to keep them happy. Putting on these snowbound soirees isn't really difficult with a little advance planning by Mother.

Try to limit the number of guests to four or six children. The best age group for this party is between five and eleven.

For the younger half of the age span, start the party directly after school and end it at six or six-thirty. The nine-to-eleven age group may prefer going home first, starting at six-thirty, and wending their way home by eight-thirty.

A telephone call a day in advance will suffice for a children's party. By not planning too far ahead, you'll be able to fairly accurately predict the weath-

er. When you call, cl[...]
hours of the party and [...]
children will be picked [...]
ered. It's best for parer[...]
guests off at your home [...]
return them. This will [...]
for you to break up th[...]
pre-set and planned time[...]

If you'd prefer that y[...]
use the back or side do[...]
to the right door with si[...]
most creative ways to po[...]
is with "Lightening" bag[...]
to make; use brown p[...]
each with an inch of s[...]
votive candle in the ce[...]
not a fire hazard becaus[...]
dles burn down, they're [...]
sand. Decorate the sac[...]
and cutouts to let t[...]
through the bag in perl[...]

Prepare a mud room i[...]
house. Spread plenty [...]
take up moisture. Provid[...]

Party settings in a hurry—Variety-store circus figures enjoy an ice cream sundae. It's a glass filled with plastic shavings and drops of food coloring topped with carnations and shaving cream.

Create a carousel with ani[...] and a ten-inch plastic foam ri[...] staple cardboard together and [...] bon and fringe. Use icing to gl[...]

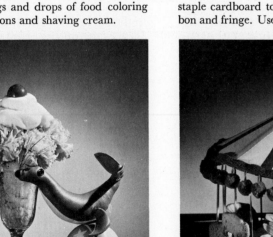

The next time you have occasion to give a shower, take it out of the "miscellaneous" class and make it something special. Choose a theme and carry it through in the decorations and refreshments. Find out the bride's or mother-to-be's favorite color or color schemes

```
❦ MENU ❧

Coffee Clouds*
Salted Almonds and Walnuts
Mints
Demitasse Coffee*
Decorated Sugar Cubes
Whipped Cream
```

and her needs—be ready to clue the guests in selecting a gift that fits the selected party theme.

One word of caution about showers—two or possibly three are enough for any one person no matter what the event. It saves wear and tear on those few who seem to receive invitations to all of the showers. The young lady herself should learn to say "no thank you" as gently, but as firmly as possible.

Make-it-paper Shower

A shower with a paper theme has unlimited possibilities. Gifts could include anything from paper towels or a cook book to an etching or print. Or guests might turn up with gift certificates to the newspaper or a favorite magazine, stationery, colorful paper hankies, napkins, and place mats, treated disposable paper, even a bride's record book or photograph album.

For entertainment, pass out sheets of newspaper, pins, and scissors and ask guests to design a wedding dress, pinning it to the bride as they go.

recipes on page 170.

Choose from a wealth of colorful paper items for decorations, ready made or hand-crafted, from mobiles to crepe paper flowers. And serve refreshments on paper plates and in paper cups. Use paper napkins and paper tablecloth, too. Cleanup is a cinch.

```
❦ MENU ❧

Grilled Bacon-wrapped Olives
Bing Cherry Mold*
Fresh Bings     Pineapple Slices
Curried Chicken Sandwiches*
Walnut Cream Roll*
Iced Coffee
```

Barbecue Shower

Order a bright, sunny day from the weatherman and rustle up a barbecue for the bride and her friends. (Be sure everyone knows it's a casual party.)

Presents? Barbecue and picnic accessories, of course. Guests may want to pool resources and get one big item like a grill, or each guest can bring a separate item. Suggestions: hot-pad mitts, barbecue utensils (long-handled fork, spoon, turner, tongs), charcoal, fire starter, grill cleanser, long matches. Other possibilities are paper plates, skewers, a long-handled frying pan, a barbecue cook book, a picnic basket, an ice bucket or picnic-size chest, or different size vacuum bottles.

And don't forget to bring along a bottle of mosquito repellent for the first gift to open—now or later.

Game-of-chance Shower

This should definitely be an evening shower so that the men can be included. Each couple brings a game. It can be your favorite "007" spy thriller or one of the old favorites like Monopoly or Scrabble. Guests should check their game selection with the hostess to avoid repetition. If the weather is warm, set up a backyard carnival using card tables for the games and a bright string of Japanese lanterns to light the scene. Afterwards the couple takes home all the games, and they have a ready-made theme for their first party.

Baby Shower

It's a grand opportunity for old friends to chat—usually you don't need games. But you might ask each guest to bring a hint on "how to raise superior children" just for fun. Prize present "from all of us": a gift certificate from a diaper service, or an infantwear shop. (Tuck the certificate in a diaper bag or fold inside a cloth or paper diaper.)

Try pink and blue paper bibs for the place mats, stuffed toys for the centerpiece, and paper booties for nut cups— and bring in a lavish dessert for the grand finale.

Bon Voyage Shower

The once-in-a-lifetime traveler will appreciate your thoughtfulness every day she's away if you shower her with travel necessities.

Packaged wet paper towels, a travel clothesline, individual packets of paper hankies, film, and fold-up plastic hangers are always welcome.

If she's going abroad, she'll be very glad to have an up-to-date currency converter, pocket money in the currency of the country she'll visit (order through your bank), guidebooks and detailed maps, a passport case, and dollar bills. Do keep the gifts lightweight.

Pastel flowers and rounds of soap make a pretty centerpiece for a bathroom shower. Use terrycloth for a tablecloth and hand towels for napkins. They're available in myriads of colors and patterns to coordinate with any scheme. Gifts may be wrapped in towels or trimmed with powder puff designs. Present ideas: accessories such as soap dish, guest towel holder, and colorful soaps.

Weights-and-measures shower features a scale as a unique centerpiece. Fill one side with a colorful bouquet and the other with small gifts. Give the bride measuring spoons, cups, scoops, steel tape measures, appliance timer, meat and candy thermometers, sewing ruler, and a letter scale. For a comment-causing dessert, decorate a long cake with frosting to resemble a yardstick.

Anniversaries are as sentimental as the scent of old lavender. Early ones are celebrated with in-the-family gifts, or casual suppers such as a paper-plate luncheon for the first year, a wood buf-

⊰ MENU ⊱

Anniversary Cake*
Coconut Ice-cream Balls*
Party Sandwiches
Mixed Nuts   Mints
Pink Punch*
Tea

A "Silver Buffet" for a 25th anniversary stars a handsome anniversary cake as a lovely centerpiece. Its colors are coordinated with those selected for the theme—pink and white. Roses and candles add color and elegance to this important event.

fet for the fifth, a tin-pan picnic for the tenth. But the extra specials—the 25th, 50th, and 75th anniversaries are candlelight-and-roses occasions.

For a major anniversary, the planning is elaborate. Friends arrange a buffet or tea honoring the couple—everyone is invited to drop in and offer congratulations. Guests may also bring gifts. Silver, gold, or white table trims and serving pieces are in order.

Invitations are most often engraved although handwritten ones are equally appropriate. The guest list includes acquaintances, friends and family of the honored couple. An anniversary tea table or buffet of small sandwiches, sweets, punch, coffee, and cake is the traditional fare. It's a good idea to provide comfortable seating for your 50th or 75th anniversary guests of honor since the hours are usually long. This is the time to decorate elaborately with all the elements custom dictates to let the couple know they're special.

← **A fifth anniversary** coffee party carries the theme in the wooden serving pieces and tableware. If guests are bringing gifts, ask that they be wrapped in specified colors, then stack them in a centerpiece-basket of wood or wicker. The light coffee-menu pictured consists of a sparkling fruit cup, coffee cake muffins, butter balls, coffee with cream floaters, mints and nuts. It's an easy fare for an after-dinner surprise.

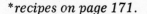

Any of the anniversaries provide an excuse for celebrating. The couple themselves may want to invite friends for dinner to help them celebrate (without telling why so the friends won't feel obligated to bring gifts) or close friends may want to surprise the couple with an after-dinner party. The party can be in any form from a cocktail buffet to a dessert and games evening. The guest list is usually limited to those who know the couple well and the invitations can be made by telephone or informal notes. With the anniversary symbols provided by tradition, decorating and gift ideas are built-in. The following table lists the traditional symbols for the special years.

Anniversary themes

1	Paper	13	Lace
2	Cotton	14	Ivory
3	Leather	15	Crystal
4	Fruit and flowers	20	China
5	Wood	25	Silver
6	Sugar and candy	30	Pearl
7	Wool or copper	35	Coral
8	Bronze or pottery	40	Ruby
9	Willow or pottery	45	Sapphire
10	Tin or aluminum	50	Gold
11	Steel	55	Emerald
12	Silk or linen	75	Diamond

*recipes on page 171.

Housewarming surprises make newcomers feel really welcome in their new neighborhood. If they are close friends you can surprise them the day they move in. Since nothing will be unpacked, plan to bring everything you'll need. Cover cardboard boxes with cheerful adhesive-backed paper for tables-for-two and bring floor pillows for chairs. An easy take-along lunch is sandwiches picked up from the corner delicatessen, fresh fruit, chips, coffee in vacuum containers, and before-dinner cocktails. Remember the ice and ice bucket, napkins, and disposable plates and glasses.

HOUSEWARMING

A warm way to say "Welcome to the neighborhood,"—that's a housewarming. New friends and neighbors reverse the traditional role and become hosts in the "guest's" new home. Or, the newcomers can give the party themselves.

When friends arrange the party it is most often a surprise. It can be the night the newcomers move in or later when they're more settled. Guests bring the edibles—sandwiches, liquids in vacuum or pop bottles, casseroles in electric containers. Other good idea bring-alongs include disposable plates, cups, utensils, napkins, and cloths, ice, an ice bucket, and bottle opener. Gifts are not mandatory, but are traditional and they're always for the house.

An "At Home" party arranged by the new homeowners takes place after they're settled. It's usually in the form of a tea, dessert coffee, or cocktail party

❧ MENU ❧

*Submarine Sandwiches**
Apples   Green Grapes
Corn Chips
Vacuum Coffee
*Toffee Bars**

and the entertainment is seeing every corner and closet of the new home.

recipes on page 171.

BON VOYAGE

Give traveling friends a happy send-off with a Bon Voyage party. A trip to a faraway place is exciting and romantic to those who rarely leave home and the honor of a going-away party will make their occasion all the more exciting.

Begin party plans by consulting the guests of honor. A well-organized family might think it fun to have the send-off the night before the departure, but others might prefer the less hectic time of a few days before. So it's best to ask.

Invitations are informal—either telephone calls, notes, or purchased invitation cards. For this event you can make clever invitations using travel or foreign country motifs.

There is no set time for this party. It could be whenever you and the travelers prefer. Invite as many or as few as you wish, as long as they all know the guests of honor well.

Themes are as easy as selecting a country where the travelers are going. You might try a Viking ship theme for the Scandinavian countries, Ionic pillars made of corrugated cardboard for Greece, or a South-of-the-Border theme complete with sombrero and vividly colored serapes. For a different approach, use a theme of unusual methods of travel. Find pictures of snowshoes, camels, a jinrickisha, a kayak, and gondola. Hang travel posters on walls and place foreign fabric runners on tables.

Plan the menu, too, by a country. You'll need only one or two dishes to suggest the theme. Or plan the entire fare to be foreign. If you have difficulty finding the right food, check a recognized cook book.

Gifts are common for a bon voyage party. Select those items which travel well and which the travelers don't have already. Unbreakable containers are always handy. Consider also books, games, passport cases, colognes or cosmetics, candy, packaged wet towels, shoe stockings, and guidebooks.

Remember, if it's the night before, to let the guests of honor get some rest before they leave. They'll appreciate your consideration and be able to enjoy the hectic departure day.

Delightful Dutch garden blooms with brilliance. The windmill is made from a half-gallon milk carton with additional pieces cut from lightweight cardboard and sticks. Add color by covering parts of the mill with paper. Build a garden of narcissus around the windmill.

A night in Venice is a romantic setting. The flower laden gondola is made with strips of cardboard bent and taped together on the prow and stern. The cardboard canopy is trimmed with gummed labels and held with matchsticks. Use striped runner for table.

Chinese junk sails peacefully on a sea of rippling bamboo mats. The vessel is constructed of narrow boxes and squares of decorative cardboard. The sail is heavy cardboard that has been bent and attached to a dowel mast. A lacquered rice bowl further sets the scene.

TEEN SPECIAL OCCASIONS

Teen-agers love parties, especially when grown-ups are not present. There is little etiquette involved, just good fun. Celebrate teen birthdays, graduations, confirmations with a party. This might be a record party, an after-the-game dance, or dinner with friends downtown. The most popular—especially with the young ladies—is the slumber party.

But before you're confronted with a dozen or more teen-age girls armed with pajamas, records, and girl talk, there are a few things you should know.

First of all, a slumber party is a very popular social event. Secondly, there is very little slumber involved. And thirdly, the party can be easy, fun, and no trouble if you'll make the necessary preplanning arrangements.

Plan to have at least one adult on hand to supervise the party. And make sure the guests' parents know that an adult will be there. If at all possible, pick up the teen-agers so their parents won't be concerned about their arriving.

Friday nights are generally best for slumber parties, since Saturday is a "no-school" day. Saturday night is not good because you may find yourself returning guests for church services at odd hours Sunday morning.

Sleeping may be the least of anyone's worries, but it's your duty to see that there is a bed, sofa, or cot space for each guest. One answer to sleeping accommodations is to leave the beds only partially made (just sheets). As guests arrive, give each one a bed roll consisting of a blanket, pillow, towels, and washcloth. That way, if guests actually want to sleep—and in comfort—they can make up a bed for themselves. You

may find the majority of guests will prefer curling up in a blanket on the floor watching TV or chatting. They'll be happier just left to their own devices rather than herded off to bed. Often teens will bring their own bed rolls.

Some extras to plan for include: a well-stocked medicine cabinet to ward off headaches or upset stomachs; some extra toothbrushes for those who may have dashed off without theirs.

The food you'll need for a slumber party may vary, but one successful plan is to have appetizers on hand during the early part of the evening and then serve a midnight buffet supper. Casseroles and oven dishes are best. They'll be ready whenever your teen-age hostess wants to serve. You might set out dinnerware, beverages, rolls, and condiments before retiring.

Stock your refrigerator with plenty of milk, soft drinks, and fruit. Have cookies, crackers and chips on hand, too, for nighttime nibblers. It might be a good idea to have popcorn fixings and candy ingredients available in case someone decides to take over the kitchen in the wee, small hours.

Plan an easy breakfast that can be set out the night before and eaten in shifts as the guests awaken. Let your hostess instruct her guests there will be fruit juice in the refrigerator, cold cereal and sweet rolls for a "serve yourself" breakfast. Or you may provide bacon and eggs for a young chef.

As far as entertainment is concerned, chances are the most popular entertainment will be girl talk and giggling, but have something else available just in case. Provide several popular games; have some teen-interest magazines and, by all means, a record player.

Try to limit records, dancing, piano playing, singing, and other noisy entertainment to the hours before midnight.

After breakfast, ask if any of your guests would like to be driven home. A general exodus should take place no later than ten o'clock.

←**Teen-agers love sweets** and they'll love an old-fashioned variety. You may not want to serve all of these in one evening, but two or three will score at the top. Sugared Nuts* are perfect for nibbling (your teen-ager can make them). Gingerbread boys on crisp apples are good party favors. Or serve cinnamon doughnuts with Hot Mulled Cider* and gingerbread squares or a spice layer cake.

*recipes on page 172.

HOLIDAY PARTIES

Everyone loves a holiday. It may be a national day such as Thanksgiving or Independence Day when all business stops or a "fun day" such as St. Patrick's Day or April Fool's Day when the day is still a working one, but is given special meaning through a long-established ethnic or historic tradition.

The holiday is especially loved by the enthusiastic party-giving hostess. The theme is set, the decorations are traditional, the menu is often established by custom, people are ready and in the mood for a party, and the day is an excuse for her to entertain.

The party plans suggested for the holidays listed in this chapter are merely ideas to give impetus to your own planning. Adapt the decorating and entertaining ideas and the menus to your mood and the occasion. Any number of parties could fit any of the holidays given. Perhaps instead of the open house on New Year's Day you'd rather hostess a brunch with the Rose Bowl parade providing the entertainment. Your decorations can remain the same as the ones suggested and your menu can be the brunch menu outlined in Chapter III—"Anytime —Party Time."

The holidays included in our party guide, in addition to New Year's Day are Valentine's Day, St. Patrick's Day, April Fool's Day, Easter, an all-occasion day, Independence Day, Halloween, Thanksgiving, and Christmas. One, two, or more party ideas are given in each case to give you a wide selection and, hopefully, to fit your particular wants for the specific holiday at hand.

Any holiday is a party day. It's fun to use your imagination in designing your decorations and in plotting your menu to fit the theme of the day and to know that your plans will be rewarded by the happy spirit of your holiday guests.

← **A Christmas dinner party** with a Danish touch in the menu and decorations gives a pleasant variation to the traditional holiday theme. Variations on any holiday theme add a special note of originality to your party atmosphere and you'll have fun thinking of new ways to do the old.

Out-of-season treats make a hit at any party and they're not too difficult to obtain. Have your grocer or fruit wholesaler order for you, but be sure to allow several weeks for the order and shipment to arrive.

Decorate for your New Year's Day party with the symbols of the day. You'll probably have Christmas decorations still up, so add just a few touches of the New Year with confetti, streamers, and perhaps a hat or two. Dress the fresh fruit with confetti picks for a colorful touch. If it's a football-watching day for the men, add a few miniature footballs, too.

NEW YEAR'S DAY

New Year's Day is the perfect time for a quiet "At Home" party. Let friends drop in for conversation and a few samples from your buffet at any time of the afternoon. It's a lovely way to start a new year and bring a close to a hectic holiday social season.

To make the day relaxed, and pleasant for you, too, plan a simple menu—perhaps eggnog and fruitcake or sandwiches. For the late visitors, a little heartier, yet still simple, menu can serve as a light supper. Have miniature steaks ready to put on the grill or broiler when guests arrive. Then serve them on French loaf buns. Have a salad chilled and waiting and a special off-season treat of fresh pineapples.

The setting of the buffet can be an unusual touch. Use a brightly painted ladder and place the tableware and food on the different rungs. Or set up the buffet in the kitchen or in a wide hallway instead of the usual dining room. You might place different courses in different locations to let guests move from area to area and group to group.

A tradition is fun to establish and you can plan your "At Home" every New Year's Day. Issue invitations verbally or by printed cards, informals, or personal stationery notes. When the word spreads, you'll be surprised and pleased at the number who drop in to call.

Another tradition for this day is a quiet luncheon with a few good friends. Again, arrange a simple, but good menu so you'll enjoy the day, too. Your main course might be a hearty soup—oyster stew, perhaps, served with a salad, crackers, and holiday dessert.

Verbal invitations are all that are needed at this informal occasion. Invite your closest friends and one new couple each year or let the events of the time plan your guest list for you.

After the lunch, spend the afternoon sipping eggnog and visiting in front of a fire or watching the ever-popular New Year's Day football games.

VALENTINE'S DAY

February 14th is a day to celebrate with all of the traditional trappings. A hearts and flowers theme is an easy one to plan for and it has a feminine quality that makes it especially popular for women-only parties.

Use Valentine's Day as an excuse for a bridge luncheon or club planning session. If you've a young friend about to be married, honor her with a tea or a bridal shower. Any of these occasions call for the prettiest and tastiest desserts you can make—all decorated in pink and white. And you'll want the prettiest table you can set. A red-red tablecloth makes a striking background for white tableware, the silver tea service, and the pink-and-white desserts. Red and white carnations and miniature hearts and birds attached to strands of florist wire make a traditional and lovely Valentine's Day centerpiece.

Pink-on-pink is elegant and perfect for a Valentine's Day celebration theme. Frost the edges of heart-, diamond-, and flower-shaped cookies with pink icing and center with tart red jelly. Top a pink-and-white marbled Angel Food cake with icing in a hue to match that of the cookies. A pink linen tablecloth is a perfect foil to a centerpiece of red roses and a punch bowl of white.

Begin your salute to St. Patrick's Day with a spicy and appealing Tomato Refresher and nibbles of cheese straws and crackers. Corned beef is a fine choice for entertaining on this day and the rest of the year, too—it offers hearty flavor and little preparation. Cook Irish potatoes, cabbage, and carrots with the meat and they'll take on savory flavor. Perfect apple pie with clover leaves of cheddar or cupcake Blarneystones frosted and covered with green-tinted coconut served with coffee are sure to be perfect toppers for this March 17th all-Irish holiday dinner.

Jumbo potatoes stand in for posies for the St. Patrick's Day centerpiece. Greenery trailed among the potatoes and beribboned clay pipes add color and another touch of the Irish.

ST. PATRICK'S DAY

Even though it's not a national holiday, St. Patrick's Day provides a happy excuse for friends to gather. The decorating theme and menu are built-in for birthday celebrations, bridge club meetings, committee luncheons, dinner parties, or informal gatherings for green beer and corned beef sandwiches. The color scheme and party motifs are traditional. Use green everywhere and be sure to decorate with plenty of shamrocks, bowlers, pipes, and pigs. You can simply suggest the theme, if you wish, by using a vase of white flowers in a mass of greenery as a centerpiece, a green or white tablecloth, and contrasting or striped napkins.

The 17th of March provides a natural theme for children's parties. Youngsters love favors of bowlers with shamrock bands or pigs pulling their jaunting carts. Sandwiches can be cut in shamrock shapes and cookies frosted with green icing. For entertainment, let them play pin the tail on the pig and invent their own dances for the Irish jig.

❧ MENU ❧

Tomato Refresher*
Corned Beef*
Irish Potatoes   Small Carrots
Cabbage
Blarneystones*
Coffee

*recipes on page 172.

APRIL FOOL'S DAY

Parties dedicated to April Fool's Day might be rare, but they do provide an imaginative reason to get together, and endless possibilities for party ideas. Spring is here and there is a reason to celebrate. Use the excuse and welcome April and spring with a luncheon. For your April Fool's prank, set your table

☙ MENU ☚

Perfect Potato Salad*
Tomato Aspic*
Cold Ham   Relishes
Bacon Cornettes*   Butter
Cherry Creme Parfaits*
Coffee

in a mis-matched theme, using as many china or pottery and silver patterns as you have available. Pull out your loudest tablecloth, then napkins in as many colors or patterns as you have and need. Even your centerpiece can be a little unconventional—leaves instead of flowers, fireplace matches (inserted into plastic foam holders) instead of candles.

Your menu can be unconventional, too, but should be appealing enough to be inviting. Perhaps this is the time to try a special recipe you've been saving for just the right moment. Foreign foods will add a novel touch that will fit right into your theme.

The April first theme can be adapted to other occasions, too. Use April Fool's Day for bazaar themes, brunches, afternoon bridge parties or bridge benefits, dessert affairs, a supper, or an evening of party games. This mismatched scheme is an easy one to arrange and is sure to attract comment.

If you choose an evening of party games, throw in a few children's games to play for the novel touch. Then serve

recipes on page 173.

snacks on unmatched paper plates—you can buy several patterns in plates and napkins from most variety stores.

Games appropriate for an April Fool's party are mind-teasing ones. If you have ready-made games, such as Jeopardy or Pass-word, that call for quick thinking, divide your guest list into teams for some friendly competition.

There are also paper-and-pencil games you can organize. Play Categories with topics to fit the day or ask guests to play anagrams by listing as many words as they can make out of April Fool's Day. Old Maid will provide a humorous children's touch for a party of adults.

Mix-and-match makes a colorful and appropriate theme for April Fool's Day. Use pottery in different patterns, glasses of different colors, tableware that doesn't match, and the wildest tablecloth and napkins you have. The centerpiece is a plate of leaves and ferns and flowers.

EASTER

Easter is a traditional time when families get together to eat. Ways to celebrate this event vary in different parts of the country. In certain areas, Easter brunch after church is popular, while some other areas favor the buffet dinner. The more traditional is the evening dinner. But no matter at which hour you serve your Easter meal, the decorations and entertainment for this annual event remain the same.

Colorful decorated eggs adorn the table along with baskets of spring flowers, and a bunny or two may poke its head out from under a blossom. For entertainment, an Easter egg hunt is almost essential for any children in the group. This is a perfect day for individual family traditions, too, such as pre-Easter egg decorating and wild-flower gathering parties, scavenger hunts for a prize or the reunion of two or three families who exchange the responsibility of hosting the dinner each year.

An Easter buffet follows the season's tradition. The Easter-egg tree, a symbol of new life, sets the stage. Blown and dyed eggs are hung by ribbon from the limbs of a manzanita branch. Ham, another Easter tradition, is the star of this dinner and to be in its best Easter finery it is beautifully glazed and trimmed with a candied orange daisy. The springy accompaniments are frilly leaf-lettuce salad, asparagus with almond topper, and parslied new potatoes. Serve hot rolls and coffee and top with Easter basket desserts of meringue shells filled with ice cream balls.

An attractively arranged buffet of perky cups and containers is a delightful way of serving the liquid refreshments at your All-Occasion Cup party. For this holiday occasion the selection is an orange tea flavored with aromatic bitters and served from a samovar, with hot buttered lemonade for a tangy pickup, Cheese Bisque* sprinkled with popcorn and accompanied by parmesan melba toast, hot mulled cider served from a grape-leaf draped glass urn, warm cranberry punch spiced with cloved oranges, and After-Dinner Mocha* with whipped cream and cinnamon sticks.

ALL-OCCASION PARTY

For an any-holiday party for any time of the year the All-Occasion Cup is adaptable and a pleasant change of pace. Cups can be made for sipping anything from soup to cider and anytime from the morning coffee to the nightcap. Why not celebrate the next holiday with a Cup party? Offer a main course of a soup, accompanied by at least one solid food such as bread and butter or crackers, then let guests help themselves to a variety of liquid refreshers. Be sure to have plenty of cups for those who'd like to sample everything.

The All-Occasion Cup party is adaptable to every season. In the summer and spring serve iced drinks, coffee, tea, and punches, and a light hot soup of a bouillon or broth base or a chilled bisque, consommé, or borsch. For the colder months, offer hearty soup, a chowder or cream soup, and hot sipping accompaniments. A few sweets, candies or cookies, are perfect go-alongs.

*recipes on page 173.

INDEPENDENCE DAY

Tradition calls for a picnic on Independence Day—whether it's in your own backyard, at a local park, at the beach, or in a meadow miles from home. Adults and children are invited to this family celebration, to feast on deliciously baked-outdoors treats and to watch the fireworks display and perhaps the local summer softball team.

Anytime of the day is the right time for your Fourth of July picnic. You and your family might enjoy a mid-morning breakfast party on the patio and perhaps later, after the parade, a neighborhood block party.

For your family breakfast, it's fun to plan a red, white, and blue scheme. A quick-to-fix, but really special breakfast of Canadian-style bacon, sugar-coated corn flakes served with a dipper of vanilla ice cream and a generous spoonful of strawberries, and a sweet roll ring made from packaged orange Danish rolls will be a big hit and will provide two of your 4th colors. Set your table with a blue tablecloth or mats, a red and white floral centerpiece, and early American print napkins. Your family will feel the spirit of Independence Day all day long.

A Fourth of July block party will take a little longer to organize than your family breakfast. If there are a large number of families living in your area, you'll probably want help in arranging this neighborhood gathering. With the help of a co-hostess, decide where the party will be, the time, how much and what food you'll need and, if it's to be potluck, and, how and when to issue the invitations.

If your yard is large enough to accommodate everyone, it would probably be the easiest and most convenient location for you to hostess the party. An alternative is a nearby park—if it's within walking distance. Transportation problems would be too cumbersome for a large group unless all agreed to charter a bus to take them to a park. The time of the party would depend on your community's organized activities. Plan to hold the event after the parade, or before the fireworks, since they do not begin until dark. Then there will be no conflict of interests.

For a picnic, plan simple foods, but be sure there is plenty of everything. When you and your co-hostess issue the invitations you can assign each family a dish to bring—or you can have the

⇜ MENU ⇝

*Hawaiian Ham Slices**
*Macaroni and Cheese Salad**
Summer Relishes
*Dilly French Loaf**
*Caramel Frosted Bars**
Fresh Fruit
Homemade Lemonade

meal catered. It is good planning, if you are not having the party catered, to arrange for some food to be prepared at the homes and cook just a part of the meal on grills. You'll save time and grill space. You'll also need to make arrangements for plenty of grills, charcoal, and cookout tools.

Little notes inviting everyone to the picnic might be the easiest way to reach everyone. Be sure to include an R.s.v.p., and the dish assignment if it's potluck. You might follow with telephone-call reminders to be sure everything is still organized. Issue the invitations at least ten days before the 4th. Families usually plan quite far in advance for their holiday activities.

For a real Independence Day atmosphere, decorate the picnic tables with red and white tablecloths (they're even available in paper), blue paper plates, napkins, and cups, and miniature flags inserted into cookies for the centerpieces on each picnic table.

recipes on page 174.

A cookout picnic couldn't be easier when you use a take-along meal like this. It's also perfect for a potluck because no one is assigned more than their share. The hostess can assume the responsibility of preparing the ham—buy enough fully-cooked hams to feed the group, then marinate thick slices in a pineapple, soy, ginger, and garlic mixture. It's cooked at the picnic and served with grilled pineapple slices atop each piece.

Several families can bring macaroni and cheese salads that can be prepared ahead and refrigerated until picnic day. Others can be responsible for the nibbles of easy-to-fix relishes—cauliflower buds, radishes, pickles, and olives.

Cook the French bread, sliced, spread with dill butter and wrapped in foil, over the coals along with the heat (start bread about 15 minutes before the ham and cook at back of grill). Then serve fresh fruit with caramel-frosted bar cookies and plenty of homemade lemonade. Your block picnic is bound to be such a success that your neighbors will demand an encore each Fourth of July.

HALLOWEEN

The night of witches and goblins is a night for children—and adults. Corn stalks, big moons, the fall nip in the air, and the general excitement of the season make party giving "something in the air." The customs and colorful traditions of Halloween make it a natural for party themes. You probably won't want to tackle all three at once, but perhaps one of the following three Halloween party ideas will appeal to you for the next 31st of October.

When your kindergartner or first grader asks to give a party, let him be the host to a Jack o' Lantern Supper. Arrange an early evening supper, time for a few games, then supervised trick or treating. For a group in this age bracket (5-7) it's best to limit the number of guests to four or six. You'll be better able to keep command, especially when they're out running from door to door. It will add to the fun and the party atmosphere if the guests come in their costumes.

It's easy to plan a menu for youngsters. Simple sandwiches, perhaps cheese on dark bread or peanut butter on white bread, can be cut into pumpkin shapes and decorated with relish features. Serve also a relish tray of carrots and celery. For special treats, serve lollipop clowns inserted into crisp apples. You can make the clowns by adding features of fruit- or mint-flavored hard candy circles to the lollipops. Add mugs of cold milk and warmed-in-the oven sugared doughnuts.

Plan one or two quick games—let each guest decorate a cutout pumpkin, make a mask from a paper bag, bob for apples, or take part in a short in-the-house scavenger hunt—then take them on their rounds. Since Halloween may be on a school night, you'll want to get everyone home as early as possible.

A costume party, with or without specific directions (such as "come as your secret desire," "come as a cowboy," or "artists and models ball") is an adult version of Halloween trick or treating. Men may balk at first, but they'll relax when they see the others in costume and will enjoy the party as much as everyone else.

Printed or hand-made invitations add to the fun of preparing and anticipating the party. They should give all necessary information—especially the fact that it's a costume party. If it is to be a large cocktail party, you won't need

❧ MENU ❧

Chili Con Carne

Dill-pickle Sticks   Olives

Double-corn Chowder*

Bread Sticks   Assorted Crackers

Caramel Apples on Sticks*

Coffee   Ice-cold Milk

RSVPs, but for a smaller group replies will be helpful to you.

The decorations don't need to be elaborate. Carve a few jack o' lanterns to sit around the room in piles of colorful fall leaves, suspend mobiles of black cats, witches, and pumpkins, and set your table with the Halloween colors of orange and black. Your centerpiece could be a bouquet of mums set into a hollowed-out pumpkin.

Plan a simple menu of cocktails and snacks—perhaps a few kinds of party sandwiches, some fresh fruit, crackers, dips, and spreads. One or two sweets will round out the menu. If you'd like a heartier menu, plan a make-your-own sandwich buffet with an assortment of cold meats, cheeses, and breads.

For the entertainment provide music for dancing, prizes for costumes, and perhaps a few party games such as Scrabble, Probe, or Tip-it. Be sure to have a photographer so you can send guests mementos of the evening.

*recipes on pages 174-175.

To follow an evening of a football game, dance, or other Halloween festivity, plan a late-late supper for a crowd. Your guests would probably like to relax a little from the earlier activities, so let them with a good meal and good conversation. You won't need any other entertainment and they'll appreciate your thoughtfulness.

For this supper party, plan just as you would for an informal dinner party. Send invitations on informals or printed Halloween invitations about 10 days in advance of the party.

Dress the house with seasonal decorations. Autumn vegetables and fruit heaped into a large bowl make an attractive centerpiece. Pumpkins, Indian corn, and dried weeds can be combined into handsome fall bouquets.

Plan your menu so that it can be ready to serve within minutes after guests arrive. Do-aheads are the easiest and quickest solution—then you just heat and serve. The menu suggestion of Chili Con Carne and Double Corn Chowder is a hearty and quick one, perfect for late night entertaining.

To save time, set your buffet or table before you leave for the evening. All that will be left to do will be to place the food in the bowls and platters.

Chili n' Chowder. What could taste better to a gang after a nippy fall-evening festivity? And this pair of hearty soups lets you feed a large group quickly and inexpensively. For best flavor and quick fixing, simmer the chili for a long time early in the day and reheat when guests arrive. Have chowder all ready to heat, too, then set them both out on a cheerful fall buffet.

THANKSGIVING

Thanksgiving is a fulfilling event. It is a time for families and friends to get together—a time when we can celebrate the togetherness and the tradition with time-honored foods. Thanksgiving is a day when all gather at Grandmother's house in the country, or at daughter's house in the city. It is a time when every house or apartment is the ideal setting for a party. Make Thanksgiving Day something special for all.

Thanksgiving is an especially appropriate day to invite away-from-home friends to your house. This is one time to treat guests as members of the family and to make them feel truly at home. Establish a Thanksgiving tradition of inviting an away-from-home friend each year or of spending the day with family friends whose relatives live too far away to come for the day.

The Thanksgiving feast is one of the most traditional of holiday fares. A few side dishes may be regional, but the turkey, cranberry sauce, and pumpkin and mincemeat pies are national. Today there are many convenience foods available to make preparing the meal easier for you. If you're planning a houseful of company, you'll probably want to take advantage of a few of the shortcuts. Then you will have more time to visit with Aunt Carrie or your college roommate who is spending the winter in your part of the country. Brown-and-serve rolls, canned and frozen vegetables, make-ahead salads, and a boned and rolled turkey roast are timesaving and tasty ideas to consider.

Not everyone has an abundance of room for a sit-down feast. The Thanksgiving buffet might be their answer. If

that's your case, you can still serve the traditional foods, but you might combine and simplify to save space. Limit your meal to three courses for easier serving and preparing, or have the dinner catered by a good delicatessen or restaurant if your kitchen is quite small. Chairs and a solid eating surface will be a necessity for everyone for this meal. Folding chairs and small folding trays

MENU

Hot Tomato Bouillon*
Roast Turkey*   Oyster Stuffing*
Whipped Potatoes   Giblet Gravy*
Gourmet Onions*
Brown-and-serve Rolls   Butter Balls
Blue-cheese Waldorf Salad

can be used in addition to card tables, coffee tables, and any other table surfaces you can find.

Decorate your house with the fruits and vegetables of winter. Baskets and cornucopias of gourds, Indian corn, dried wheat, apples, and pears make colorful and appropriate centerpieces and bouquets. A glass or porcelain turkey, if you have one, should reign on the mantel or table. Children's decorations are always welcome for the day. Hang that Pilgrim scene or cutout turkey in a place of honor.

The table and buffet should be dressed in harvest colors to complete your theme. Browns, golds, reds, yellows, and oranges in accessories will complement your winter centerpiece and your Thanksgiving menu.

The ingredients for this happy day are simple—combine family members of all ages, good friends, and an abundance of food. The result will be a day for which everyone will be thankful.

←**Scrubbed pine and pewter** and a regally-perched turkey centerpiece set a traditional mood on this Thanksgiving table. The fare, too, is traditional with the roast turkey starring for the day. Butter-browned peach halves and spiced crabapples nesting in sprigs of parsley add a simple, but colorful touch to the turkey platter—and they take little fuss in the kitchen, don't hinder the carving.

*recipes on page 175.

CHRISTMAS

One of the busiest and happiest times of the entire year is Christmastime. It's the busiest because it's packed with shopping, baking, wrapping, decorating, and entertaining. It's the happiest because it's the time of year we spend with all those we love the best. That is why the holidays are such a marvelous time to entertain—we're already in a festive mood and we want to share the Christmas spirit with everyone.

Planning holiday parties should be easier than planning for any other time of the year. The theme is built in—it's Christmas. Party possibilities centered around the traditional festivities are numerous. For the family, plan a special Christmas Eve supper; for weekend guests, a holiday breakfast; for young people and their companions, a tree-trimming and carol-singing evening; for the neighborhood and business friends, an open house; and for best friends and family, an elegant dinner party.

The holiday dinner

Whether you plan a dinner for your family on Christmas day, or a gathering of a few close friends on the 22nd, the dinner party is a popular part of all holiday entertaining. Little informal buffet dinner parties are perfect for this busy season. The hostess who is swamped with activities, or the one who is employed will appreciate the convenience of a sit-down buffet dinner party. This party can be easily adapted to our modern informal life with yet the right touch of elegance and formality.

For this rush-rush season, select a three or four course meal with do-ahead

← **The ever-favorite holiday dinner** begins with a chill-warming course of Christmas Cheese Chowder, assorted crackers, and hard rolls—all made to look their festive best on a traditionally decorated table. A must for this type of table arrangement is a low centerpiece to allow conversation without neck craning across the table. The slender tapers add the true touch of holiday elegance.

items. In this holiday menu, the first course of Christmas Cheese Chowder can be prepared before the dinner date and reheated before the meal. The eggnog desert can be kept frozen for days.

Begin the evening of the dinner with cocktail treats in the living room, giving guests a chance to relax while the hostess is placing the soup on the table and the main course on the buffet.

MENU

Christmas Cheese Chowder*
Assorted Crackers   Hard Rolls
Standing Rib Roast
Yorkshire Pudding
Broccoli with Easy Hollandaise*
Wine
Frozen Eggnog*
Demitasse

When the soup course has been completed, clear the dishes and let guests help themselves at the buffet. The host may help by serving the roast. Serve the dessert at the dining table and the demitasse in the living room. The hostess pours for each guest from a coffee service placed on a low coffee table.

Good conversation, low music, and the good food are the entertainment for the evening. Your party is sure to be a success because you'll be an organized, relaxed, and happy hostess enjoying it all with those you love.

Trimming the tree

The impromptu nature of an evening of tree-decorating and carol-singing lends freedom for casual entertaining. The informal supper party fits perfectly into the mood of the evening.

Unexpected guests are always welcome at this gathering. The wise hostess will plan an expandable main dish such as the steaming Chili Con Carne suggested in the menu. The extra voices and hands will add even more gaiety to the singing and decorating.

The serving hour can also be flexible. Eat early in the evening before the decorating begins, or eat as late as you like (be sure to have plenty of snacks on hand). The dining hour will depend on when the guests are hungry. The food should be ready to heat and serve in minutes no matter when the dining time.

Everything can be prepared ahead and stored in the refrigerator. Just heat the cheese triangles and chili before serving time. All that's left to do is set the table, put out the serving dishes, and wait for your guests.

Holiday open house

Now is the time to deck the table with the traditional specialties of the season —your favorite cookie and candy treats, a sparkling punch, an attractive tray of assorted cheeses and crackers, a fruit-cake, and salted nuts. Open your house to neighbors and friends and friend's

friends, business and social acquaintances, aunts, uncles, and cousins. You'll have an afternoon filled with cheerful holiday chatter and warm laughter.

The open house requires much advance preparation in the way of baking and arranging, but the day itself will

⊰ MENU ⊱

Chili Con Carne*
Carrot Curls   Stuffed Celery*
Cherry Tomatoes
Crisp Cheese Triangles*
Christmas Lime Parfait Pie*
Eggnog*

run smoothly and easily. Plan ample supplies of food, stagger the party hours on the invitations, ask one or two friends to help replenish trays, and enjoy visiting with your open house guests.

Small intimate groupings around card tables and low coffee tables invite good supper conversation and easy mixing. Tables for four can be arranged early in the afternoon away from the traffic pattern of decorators and carolers. If unexpected guests arrive, simply add another table.

*recipes on pages 176-178.

Tree trimming hints—have all of the tree baubles unpacked and out when guests arrive. If you have a plan in mind, write it on a slip of paper and tack it near the tree. You might ask guests to bring their favorite Christmas record to play and sing along with while they're decorating.

Open house serving ideas will help you say "Happy Holidays" at your house. Mincemeat Turnovers* (below) are wonderful when served warm and are extra special when accompanied by cubes of sharp cheddar cheese. It's easy to short-cut the job by using packaged piecrust mix and prepared mincemeat.

Your party table will require a very "Christmasy" centerpiece, whether elaborate or subtly simple. For the easiest of all, yet pretty too, set an oversized red candle into a bowl of greens and cones.

Pinwheel Sandwiches* and Deviled Ham Dip* (below) add color and design to your table. Boldly seasoned braunschweiger and refreshing watercress-cream cheese pinwheels are simple do-aheads. And so is the dip. Serve well-chilled tomato juice or vegetable cocktail as a perfect companion, both in flavor and color.

Trays of nuts around the room, along with a supply of nutcrackers and picks, add another flavor and texture besides the cracking enjoyment.

Warm treats on a wintry afternoon are a welcome addition to an open house menu (above). These Ham Nuggets*, spiked with green onion, have a bright holiday look and an interesting texture from finely chopped water chestnuts. Crisp crackers and cheese-filled celery make flavorful accompaniments.

Napkins can be made from sewing trim and cotton fabric. Sew a border of narrow banding, then invent your own center pattern.

Hours in the kitchen are out when you serve Coffee Royal Eggnog* and Noel Bars*. They are an easy way to serve a crowd and make it a real holiday party. When the punch bowl is as pretty as this one, it can easily serve as your centerpiece. Just surround it with tree ornaments and sprigs of fresh greenery. A corsage of greens and Christmas bows gives even the ladle a holiday glow. Another good serving idea—individual trays to hold the treats.

Turn Christmas Eve supper over to your children (with a little beforehand preparation, of course). It's easy for the kids to make the sandwiches and the Tomato-Chicken-Rice Combo.

All the soup recipe calls for is ready-made soup in cans and water. The youngsters will enjoy their active role in the evening's festivities and learn how to be gracious hosts and hostesses.

Christmas Eve supper

Whether your family opens gifts on Christmas Eve or Christmas morning, everyone is sure to be weary, excited, and hungry that evening before Christmas. A welcome way to calm them, yet leave them with enough appetite for tomorrow's feasting, is to treat them to a tureen supper. Choose a hearty soup or chowder that needs little else to make

Holiday breakfast

Whether you have holiday overnight guests from out of town or family members only, you'll want to compliment them with your best on Christmas morning. A holiday demands special treats, even for those who settle for toast and coffee the rest of the year.

A favorite at Christmastime is a festive holiday bread dressed up with can-

MENU

Tomato-Chicken-Rice Combo*
Crackers   Small Sandwiches
Carrot Curls   Celery   Olives
Fresh Fruit
Cookies
Milk   Coffee

MENU

Orange Juice
Assorted Cereal   Cream
Swiss Baked Eggs*
Grilled Ham and Sausage
Christmas Morgen Brot*   Butter
Coffee

a meal—crackers, bread or small sandwiches; crisp relishes; fresh fruit and cookies; assorted cold drinks and coffee. It's simple for busy you, both in the preparation and in the cleanup after the evening meal is over.

Preparing for this family night supper requires little effort on your part. Most soups and chowders can be fixed ahead of time, several days if you like, and heated through at the last moment. Sandwiches can be made just before supper, or in the afternoon and stored in plastic wrap in the refrigerator. Chill the relishes in the afternoon, wash the fruit and arrange into an elegant centerpiece. Set the table in Christmas reds and greens. It's a meal you can prepare without any help, except that of your willing youngsters or visitors. They can help you make pretty carrot curls and delicate celery strips.

Cleanup will also be a breeze. The only dishes you'll have will be the soup spoons, plates, bowls, and serving pieces. A tureen supper will give you a chance, too, to relax on Christmas Eve and make your holiday even merrier.

died fruit, walnut halves, and a frosty icing. That can be the special treat included in a help-yourself breakfast of Swiss Baked Eggs in individual casseroles, orange juice, assorted cereal, grilled ham and sausage, and coffee.

The help-yourself breakfast does not need to take hours of your Christmas morning. The holiday bread can be baked the day before or even earlier and frozen, then warmed and iced that morning. The baked eggs served in individual ramekins, can be cooking while you grill the ham and sausage.

Space-savers may be important, too, at this busy time. Try using a lazy-Susan for cereals, sugar, cream, and little extras. A small table for the coffee service will ease congestion at the main buffet area. Silver, plates, napkins, and juice can be placed, before the meal, with the place settings.

If time allows, arrange the buffet the night before. Cover it with a table runner and arrange a centerpiece of candles. The arrangement could be planned to keep as part of your holiday decorations, long after the food is gone.

recipes on page 179.

SPECIAL SITUATION ENTERTAINING

Every hostess is confronted at some time by special situation entertaining. It could be one of many types —entertaining in a small space, on a limited budget, in a hurry, or even out of town. If the hostess is smart, she will have prepared for the event, will have given as much thought and planning to the special situation as to any other party. All too often, the hostess finds herself unprepared for these situations.

Yet, think of the time and money that can be saved, the headaches that can be avoided, if you have a blueprint for entertaining in any situation. These parties can turn out to be as much fun as any when you have them totally under control well in advance.

One good way to be prepared for an emergency party is to rely on and use your hostess notebook to record entertaining formulas you have found successful in the past and which can be adapted for special situations. These little formulas need not be elaborate and could include recipes and menus you have tried and which your guests have enjoyed; games that get a party going; decorative themes and table settings that cost little and can be assembled in a hurry; snacks and buffet meals that can be prepared in a jiffy; low cost food ideas for budget entertaining; and seating and serving arrangements for dining and entertaining in a small space. If you add faithfully to the book as you entertain more, you will find that you have entertaining recipes and party ideas for almost every unexpected situation and can successfully cope with anything that might arise.

But remember, it's your attitude that really counts. If you approach the situation with self-confidence you will find the challenge of solving any emergency situation both exciting and stimulating.

← **Impromptu settings** are easy to arrange for special situation entertaining. A round table and four chairs, usually used for card and other games, easily becomes an intimate dining ensemble in a living room. The wood-cloth folding screen helps separate the dining area from the rest of the room.

LIMITED SPACE ENTERTAINING

Young marrieds, mature families whose children are in college or have families of their own, bachelor-girls and -men may have one thing in common—limited space. Whether an apartment or a little house, there's little room for entertaining. This lack of space need not prevent anyone from entertaining successfully. It is fun to take friends out to a restaurant on occasion, but there is something much more intimate and hospitable about entertaining friends at home. If you're worried about entertaining in what may seem to you to be a much-too-small space, this section is designed to show you that few spaces are really too small for entertaining when you plan ahead.

Planning is of primary importance when space is at a premium; and imagination and ingenuity are the tools of your success. Once you have planned your guest list and the food and beverages you will serve, think about the atmosphere and surroundings. A cleverly decorated table, candlelight, pretty accessories, and attractively arranged food all combine to create the mood that counterbalances the lack of space. And everyone appreciates something that has been prepared with loving care.

Planning

If you have a very small dining area or no dining room and only a small living room, then you must limit your dinner guests to either four or six. To invite more would be disastrous. It is better to entertain twice in one week than crowd too many people into a too-small dining space for a dinner party.

You can extend the guest list by two or four more if you are serving only drinks and cocktail snacks. There will be no problem of space for table-dining or seating since guests most often stand at a party of this nature.

The key to entertaining in postage-stamp space is strategic planning and your own execution of those plans. If you are well organized, then your party will run smoothly, and the only way to be really organized in a small space is to do all preparations well in advance of the guests' arrival.

Drinks

It's a good idea to set up a bar in the corner of the living room or in a den or other room rearranged just for the party so that your host can serve drinks easily and not take up needed room in the kitchen. If you do not have a suitable sideboard, table, or dinner cart for this purpose, you can make good use of a folding table. Cover the table with a pretty linen, vinyl, or paper cloth and add a small bowl of flowers if you have enough room. When using another room, make use of the furniture in that room. A desk or chest that is protected with trays or cloths can be the bar.

Bottles of liquor, soft drinks, and mixes, glasses, mixing and measuring equipment, and a bucket of ice should be placed on a large tray or two trays so that the host has a solid surface to work on. Trays save the tabletops, too, in case of spills. Except for the ice, all of the bar equipment can be set up early in the day or even the day before.

Snacks

Snacks should be limited to small dishes and tiered serving trays of easy-to-handle finger foods which can be put out on the coffee and end tables before guests arrive. It's best to keep all of the snack items small—nuts, chips, diced cheeses, cherry tomatoes, sliced carrots and

Draperies installed on the curve create a dining → area at one end of this apartment living room. The drapery room divider also serves to create a small foyer near the front door. The round glass table accommodates four guests with ease. For an improvised dining arrangement away from the kitchen and from any sideboard or buffet surfaces, a dinner cart for the hostess is a necessity.

celery, halves of hard-boiled eggs, and small fingers of toast covered with salmon, cream cheese, anchovies, or meat spreads, and bowls of dips.

If you are not serving food later and want to serve more substantial hot snacks with drinks, you can be more ambitious. Hot cocktail sausages, meatballs, shrimp, and liver and bacon on cocktail sticks are ideal, as are hot pastry cases filled with mushrooms, cheese, or chopped meat. You can buy small pastry cases at most supermarkets. You simply add fillings and pop them into the oven. Limit your hot snacks to one or two and those that can be prepared ahead of time and reheated. You'll need your kitchen space for your dinner preparation.

Meals

Serving food in a small space is not half as difficult as it sounds if you plan carefully. The trick is to think out your menu—cook food that can be served and handled easily. It's also an excellent idea to arrange for dishes that can be prepared well in advance of guests' arrival to save you from trips in and out of the kitchen. Cold assorted meats are an obvious choice; they need no advance preparation at all except arrangement on the serving tray. Garnishings such as slices of tomato, sprigs of parsley and watercress, radishes and slices of cucumber add to the attractiveness of the tray. A good mixed green salad, potato, and other cold salads, go well with cold meats. If you prefer you can serve hot vegetables which are easy to cook at the last minute. Baked potatoes are also little trouble.

If you want to serve a hot meal to your guests, it is much simpler to choose a main dish that can be cooked in the afternoon and reheated later or one which can be made days ahead and frozen. A spicy chicken stew, sliced chicken in cream sauce, beef in wine sauce, curried lamb, chili con carne, paella, chicken potpie, beef and kidney pie are ideal and they can be served with rice, baked potatoes, a side dish of noodles or mixed green salad. It's

really much better to avoid very fancy dishes or ones that need individual attention such as roasts of meat or fowl (carving can present a problem in a small space). Assorted cheeses and fresh fruit go well with almost any main dish and are a good choice for dessert. Neither require advance preparation and both can be set out on the buffet before guests arrive. Alternatives would be ice cream, fresh fruit salad, thawed frozen berries, or chocolate cake.

One-platter meals save room, too, both on your table and in the kitchen at cleanup time. Place vegetables around the main dish and garnish with parsley. Eliminate the large salad bowl by placing the salads in the individual bowls and putting them at each place setting on the dining table.

The buffet

A meal served buffet-style is the perfect solution to dining in a small space. There is a certain informality about a buffet meal which we all like and enjoy and it presents fewer headaches to the hostess. The table for the food, plates, napkins, silverware, and glasses can be set up in the morning. A floor length cloth, a centerpiece, and candles add to the decorative effect of the room and enhance the food.

You can set the table at any time during the day, but do not bring the food out until just before the guests are due. If you are serving hot dishes, bring them out only when you are ready to eat. It's an excellent idea to have a stack of small trays at one end of the table so guests can use them to carry their food back to their chairs. It is also more comfortable for guests to balance a tray rather than a small plate on their laps. An even better idea, if you can afford it, is to buy a set of small folding tables made of metal or wood. You can find them at most department or hardware stores and they are relatively inexpensive. In effect, they are small trays on legs and you can place one next to each guest's chair to make buffet dining more comfortable. Simply bring them out just before supper is to be served and remove them later. Fold-

When floor space is limited, dinner or supper served buffet-style solves many problems. At the end of this living room a simple wooden board resting on two old-fashioned sawhorses receives a "banquet" camouflage with the use of a brocade-appearing linen cloth and a floral centerpiece. The wooden board and sawhorses are easy to dismantle and store after the party is over.

ing or stack stools are a boon to the hostess with little room, too. Bring them out only for the party, then return them to their storage spot.

Guests help themselves at a buffet meal. The hostess always suggests seconds and collects the plates after the meal is finished. If you are serving wine, beer, or other beverages, the host fills the glasses and hands one to each guest as he moves away with his plate. Sometimes it's fun to set up your buffet table in the kitchen, if you have enough room, and if you have spruced up the kitchen after preparing the food. Guests help themselves at the kitchen table and take their food back to the living room. If you plan to arrange your buffet table in the kitchen, make it just as pretty as you would if it were in the living room. Add a floor-length cloth, a centerpiece, and candles to give it a festive party air and color-coordinate it to your theme.

Sit-down dinner

The only successful way to serve a sit-down dinner in a home with no dining area is to create an area within the living room. If you have a dining table and chairs, most of your problems are solved; if you do not, you will have the problem of creating the dining facilities.

A large piece of solid plywood resting on two horses and covered with a floor-length cloth makes a perfectly usable table and even unmatched chairs can be given uniformity with the addition of matching cushions. You can make or purchase cushions relatively inexpensively.

Alternatively, if you intend to give a large number of sit-down dinners, it's

Bright vinyl cloth completely disguises a plywood table with removable screw-in legs. It's a perfect table for entertaining. These wicker chairs receive extra comfort and looks, too, with the addition of foam cushions covered in vinyl. The whole ensemble makes an ideal dining set in the corner of a living room. When extra space is needed, the table is dismantled.

The garden-like theme of the room is also carried out in the temporary furnishings. Garden chairs would be equally at home entertaining on the patio and the table can be set up anywhere.

worth investing in a large round plywood table top and three screw-in legs. The top and legs are available at most hardware stores and the separate pieces are easy to put together and dismantle later for storing. The unpainted surface is totally disguised with the addition of a long, circular cloth. Folding metal or wooden garden chairs, gaily painted and cushioned, provide adequate seating with the "do-it-yourself" table.

Of course, serving food at a sit-down dinner in a small space requires some ingenuity. If you do not have a side table with an ample surface for hot dishes, your best solution is a two- or three-tier dinner cart. After guests have been seated, wheel out the food-laden cart and place it next to your chair. Pass each dish around the table family-style for guests to help themselves. Ask guests to pass their plates to you when the meal is finished and place the empty dishes on the bottom tier of the dinner cart as you receive them. The cart not only serves as your sideboard and maid, but also saves you countless steps, time to be with guests, and valuable energy.

After dessert has been served, offer guests their coffee away from the dinner table—perhaps the coffee service can be set up on a coffee table in the living room area. Then you can quickly stack up empty serving and dessert plates on the cart and wheel it out. Friends should not be allowed to help when you're working in crowded conditions and it is best to clear away as quickly and quietly as possible. The tablecloth, candles, and centerpiece are, of course, left where they are for the rest of the party.

Atmosphere

The appearance and atmosphere of your home will contribute to the feeling of "smallness" or spaciousness. You may want to remove all dainty objects and bric-a-brac for the party. Have just a few large ash trays where necessary. If you've invited a large group for a cocktail party, and if you don't mind rearranging your furniture, move one or two pieces which could obstruct traffic to another room. Push the dining table against the wall for the buffet or cocktail snack service.

Guests will feel the tension if you are apprehensive and edgy. Above all, don't apologize for your situation. If you are relaxed and confident, few will notice or even care about the lack of space. A clever hostess knows her party limitations and plans so well even in emergencies that she seems to have no problems or "special situation" at all.

LIMITED-BUDGET IDEAS

Experienced hostesses know how to entertain on a limited budget—and do it well. Experienced hostesses or not, we all like a challenge and there is something particularly challenging about using ingenuity, imagination, and skill instead of money. Certainly entertaining on a limited budget requires all three attributes. The results of creating "something from nothing" are particularly satisfying and worth the effort.

You must have the right attitude about entertaining on a tight budget to make your party a success. Don't expect elaborate results, for if you do, you will be disappointed. But do set a realistic standard of quality, and know your expenditure limitations.

When you are working with a small budget, it's best to itemize everything you will need to buy. Food and beverages, your primary considerations, must be listed first. If you find you have allotted most, or all, of your budget on these essentials, you will have to compromise on the decorations. Use your imagination and ingenuity to create your decorations from what you already have or can pick up in a garden, from the surrounding countryside, or on beaches. There are numerous natural things you can use as accessories on your table or on walls and often these gifts from nature are more effective than decorations you can purchase from party shops.

Budget decorating ideas

Little decorating ideas and notions add enormously to the overall atmosphere of a party whether it's large or small, informal or formal. For some reason, food

Paper magic works economic wonders for a party. This summer luncheon setting sparkles in yellow and red floral paper plates and mats that can work all year round, indoors or out. To carry out the theme, repeat the colors in the tablecloth, also available in paper, matching napkins, and individual flowers, and with bright tissue paper used to swaddle the plant centerpiece.

always seems to look and taste better when it is on an attractively decorated table in a room with a festive air. It's a nice idea to carry the decorative theme from the table into the rest of the room if you can. If you cannot continue the theme by using matching items, then co-ordinate the colors of flowers, candles, and other accessories.

Nature provides many beautiful objects that you can collect and incorporate into your party accessory grouping. A piece of driftwood picked up on a beach, or an old piece of gnarled branch can become the base for a centerpiece for a dinner, luncheon, or buffet table. If the wood is particularly attractive in shape, grain, and color, it can stand alone between four tall candles. If it needs embellishing, tack bright paper flowers all over it. You can purchase these for pennies in a variety store or you can make them yourself. Affix tiny flowers (lilies-of-the-valley, forget-me-nots, and daisies) so that they seem to be growing out of the branch. Achieve a coordinated look with the rest of your scheme by picking up the flower colors in paper napkins, paper plates, and candles.

The same piece of wood can be equally as effective if it is placed in the center of a table and surrounded by mounds of freshly scrubbed vegetables —parsnips, carrots, onions and potatoes as a base, tomatoes, cucumber, squash, radishes, and green and red peppers as a second, higher tier.

A mixture of seashells and pieces of coral attractively arranged around the base of two candle holders is another idea for a dinner-table centerpiece. Use the same shells to make a wall around any small vase of fresh flowers.

If you are handy with scissors and crepe paper, make your own selection of exotic jungle blossoms which are gay, decorative accessories in any party room. If you want to be daring, make the flower-heads super-size and attach them to extra-long wire stems. Then arrange them in wicker wastepaper baskets on the floor. The effect will be that of small jungle trees growing around the room. Again, the flowers can be color

matched to table linen and other party accessories. Mix your paper flowers with large bunches of real leaves.

Candlelight has always been effective in creating a romantic party atmosphere in any room. Today there are hundreds of shapes, sizes, designs, and colors available. Sometimes the more elaborate candles can be costly. If your budget won't allow the elaborate ones, you can achieve a striking effect by using plain white household candles in a variety of novelty holders. They'll look charming scattered around the room and you can make imaginative holders yourself from items you already own.

Any wine, champagne, or unusually shaped bottle can be used as a candle holder. They're ideal in a family room and for informal parties. Any unusual glass dish, bowl, or small vase will also make a perfect candle holder as will pretty cream jugs, small copper molds, or unusual copper cooking utensils. To make a candle balance in an unusual container, cut a medium-size potato in half, scoop out a small hole in the rounded portion, and insert the candle into the hole. Fit flat side of the potato face down into the container. The candle will stand quite securely in place. Once you have placed the candle in its container, cover the base with handfuls of tiny seashells mixed with glass beads, real flowers (heads only), artificial flowers, pieces of gnarled wood, sand, or white gravel. Glass bowls make especially charming holders when filled with colorful stones, shells, beads, or flowers.

To carry your decorative theme throughout the house, you may have to allow a little more in your party budget for the accessories. By planning ahead you can economize in another area.

South-of-the-border theme

The Mexican theme is a popular low-budget party idea. Both food and accessories are low priced. The decorative accessories are easy to assemble and make. Paper flowers in straw baskets add a profusion of color to tables or room corners and, combined with ordinary household candles in wine bottles, they set the party mood. Odd lengths of vividly colored felt cut into strips and trimmed with inexpensive ball fringe make excellent table runners. The perfect centerpiece for the table is a straw basket filled with real or artifical vegetables. Copper cooking utensils, wooden salad bowls, earthenware, and brightly colored modern ovenware are ideal for salads and other food and they add to the rustic mood. Any Mexican or Spanish hat, preferably a large straw one, makes a good wall decoration or a centerpiece for a large buffet table. Trim it with ribbon and bunches of artificial flowers.

No-room dining is made simple with additional "pull-up" seating—a saving idea for the young in heart and thin in pocketbook. The square benches are ideal for casual seating.

Another budget decorating idea—the unique "off-centerpiece"—a semi-circle of flowering plants in clay pots and their own saucers is color coordinated to the rest of the setting.

Oriental theme

Japanese and Chinese themes are easy to re-create in your own home for the same reasons as the south-of-the-border theme. The accessories are easy to make or obtain at little cost and the party food can be budget cost, too.

Most novelty shops sell colorful, inexpensive imports from Hong Kong and Japan today and many of these can be the springboard for your decorative theme. Large and miniature paper parasols, paper lanterns, paper wall scrolls, brightly colored china rice bowls, chop sticks, and even paper kimonos and robes are relatively inexpensive and won't make a very large hole in your budget. Since Oriental flower arrangements are rather austere, all you need are several bud vases or tall, slender vases containing one or two blooms.

Overall decorating themes such as the south-of-the-border and oriental ones are particularly successful outside in gardens or patios and in family rooms. So don't limit your party decorating or your party giving to the living and dining areas of your home. You can decorate all over the house when you use your imagination and objects at hand—even on a tight budget.

Let imagination and a few simple accessories create an ingenious centerpiece. Bunches of red onions (from a supermarket or vegetable stand) surrounding matching red candles glow even more with the addition of tiny strands of Christmas tree lights entwined among them. A floral cloth picks up the blues and greens of the room and makes a perfect backdrop for the centerpiece.

EASY FOOD IDEAS

When you are entertaining in limited space or on a limited budget, easy food ideas are important. To succeed they must be well prepared and attractively presented. Tricks in planning and preparing easy menus will make you a clever and popular hostess.

Cocktail snacks

There are many tasty cocktail snacks which you can make in a jiffy.

Vegetable platters are crisp and fresh-tasting. Fill the center of a large glass bowl with a small shrimp dish or fruit cocktail goblet filled with shaved ice. Arrange slices of celery, olives, and radishes around one ice-filled dish, and carrot slices, endive, melon slivers, cherry tomatoes, and baby plum tomatoes around a second one.

Hot snacks can vary from tiny cocktail sausages to baby meatballs. Serve them with a dip (mustard or horseradish with sausages, hot tomato sauce with meatballs). Skewer liver, bacon, and chestnuts on a toothpick for another snack. Small pastry cases can be filled with hot cheese, shrimp, chopped mushrooms, or tiny crab pieces and can be popped into the oven at the last minute.

Marinated artichoke hearts and chopped clams are also good. Serve canned artichoke hearts on a cocktail stick. They need no embellishment. Spread a mixture of the chopped clams and sour cream on crackers or toast.

Sandwiches and salads

Serve substantial and unusual sandwiches and a salad for an easy supper. King club sandwiches are simple to prepare and are tasty and filling. Use white bread toast, slivers of chicken, turkey, and ham, crumbled bacon, slices of tomato, onion, lettuce leaves, and mayonnaise for each sandwich. Build in layers with toast, mayonnaise, lettuce, chicken, and tomato on the first; toast, mayonnaise, ham, onion, and bacon on the second; turkey, onion, bacon, tomato, lettuce, and mayonnaise on the third; and top with a fourth slice of toast. Skewer the finished sandwich with an extra-long cocktail stick.

Scandinavian open sandwiches can be a whole-meal feast. Use a variety of breads and fill with cold meats, cheeses, tomatoes, cucumbers, onions, and sliced eggs. Garnish each open sandwich with a sprig of parsley or watercress and an attractively cut pickle.

Salads go well with both king club and open sandwiches. Try chunky quarters of peeled cucumber in thin sour cream flavored with pepper, salt, dill, and paprika or a salad of canned chick peas, sliced onion, pepper, salt, and oregano leaves in an oil and vinegar dressing. Let the pea salad chill for at least a day before serving.

Have a variety of relishes and pickles to serve with sandwiches and salads. They add to the flavor of the food and give the buffet a more substantial look.

Garnishings can be as different as you want to make them. Top an open sandwich with a round of pineapple and a cocktail cherry, a slice of fresh orange, apple, or pear, a ring of apple or onion fried in batter, with a thin slice of melon or with whole berries.

Simple hot dishes can often replace sandwiches at a buffet supper, particularly in winter. Check your cook books for casserole dishes that look particularly taste-tempting and which call for simple, low-cost ingredients.

It often happens that you must give a more substantial dinner or supper than the ones mentioned—and still do it in a special situation. The main course must be your first consideration and the first and third courses can be very simple. Sometimes a good foreign dish can be the basis for this kind of dinner. Many international dishes are simple to prepare and the ingredients readily available. If you do serve a foreign dish always serve a simple, well-known first course and a popular dessert.

ENTERTAINING IN A HURRY

Every hostess has nightmares about one particular type of entertaining—the last-minute party. But none of us can avoid those "hastily-thrown-together" parties, since they are bound to occur at intervals during the year. It might be your husband who calls up and says he is bringing home a couple of colleagues, visiting firemen, or even more important, the boss; or teen-age children who ask to bring a group of friends home with them; even out-of-town friends who are in the neighborhood and want to "drop in."

But no matter what the circumstances are, you as the hostess are expected to be ready and prepared and smiling at the door, even if you receive only an hour's notice. As a matter of fact, in-a-hurry entertaining can be lots of fun, as long as you are prepared, and in command of the situation. And that's not as difficult as it sounds.

Of primary importance is the manner in which you greet your unexpected guests, and the atmosphere in your home when they arrive. Most people who are being brought home unexpectedly realize the work it places on you, and are often slightly embarrassed. You will only make them feel worse if you are panicky, harassed, or unsmiling. Do be charming, friendly and unhurried. Let your house reflect charm, too. Light a few candles, put records on the stereo, and turn off the television. There is nothing worse for guests than to feel they have interrupted your evening.

Once you have spruced up the room where you will entertain and made it as comfortable as possible, set out a tray of drinks—beer, mixed drinks, or soft drinks, glasses and ice. Put the tray in the room so your husband can serve the moment he arrives with your guests, and also entertain them if you have to be in the kitchen. Your next step is to tidy your bathroom, or guest bathroom, put out fresh towels and soap. When you have completed these three chores, give your own make-up and hairdo a quick touch up and change your clothes. The added self-confidence will carry over into your welcome.

If you are quick, you will have been able to accomplish these tasks in half an hour. This leaves you another half an hour to prepare snacks or more substantial food. Easy-to-prepare cocktail snacks include dishes of fresh vegetables; squares of cheese and a cocktail onion on cocktail sticks; hot cocktail sausages or meatballs; hard boiled eggs spread with mayonnaise; and the usual nuts, crackers, and chips. As soon as these are ready, put them out in the living room so that guests have something to nibble on with their drinks.

Giving guests a more substantial meal can present problems, if you don't have a lot of food in the refrigerator, or a good supply of canned goods. Cold soup in summer, or hot soup in winter, is always a good standby, served with crackers or hot rolls and butter. After the soup you can serve cold meats and a mixed salad, pancakes filled with canned creamed chicken, or a fluffy cheese omelet with toast.

King club sandwiches and open sandwiches (mentioned earlier in this chapter) can be made from the everyday foodstuffs you might have in the refrigerator, or from canned foods; a chef's salad is a dish that's easy to prepare from existing food, and you can add sliced cheese, hard boiled eggs, strips of fried bacon, and diced ham to make it more filling.

Spaghetti and noodles are good staples to keep in stock, since they are quick to prepare, and can be served with a hot meat sauce, melted cheese, or a thick tomato paste. Rice is another useful standby, which you can serve with shrimp and crab (canned) heated in a tomato or cream sauce.

If you know you will be doing lots of "in-a-hurry" entertaining it's smart planning to keep a good supply of canned food in stock—soups, fish, ham and vegetables, or frozen foods, which can be whipped up into an appetizing meal.

ENTERTAINING OUT OF TOWN

Country or beach weekends can be lots of fun, even for you, the busy hostess, if you have planned well in advance. If you are inviting friends to stay at your weekend country cottage, beach cottage, cabin by the lake, or any other weekend vacation home, and have no outside help, you must be well organized, or you will spend all weekend cooking in the kitchen or making beds.

If your "second" home is used only on weekends or for special occasions, it is best that you arrive one day or half-a-day in advance of your guests, so that you can prepare for their arrival.

Organizing your time alone at your weekend place allows you to accomplish many of the chores that would eat into your time with your guests. The house can be cleaned and that "closed-up" chill taken off it, by opening windows and doors for airing purposes, lighting fires or turning on central heating, whichever is necessary. Your next important chore is checking the refrigerator, freezer, and store of canned goods, as well as the bar. Ordering your food and drink should be done immediately, and the food stored away before your guests arrive. It's also a good idea to defrost frozen foods you will need at this time, and plan the weekend menus.

In summer, salads, cold platters, fruit, cheese, fish dishes if you are near a beach, cold meat pies and a roast are the ideal dishes to serve. It's worthwhile making some of them in advance, so that they can be simply taken out of the refrigerator when you need them. In winter, stews, rice dishes, and roasts are good, and again you can prepare some before your guests arrive.

The guest room(s) should be aired, cleaned, and prepared in readiness for guests long before they arrive. After you have made the bed(s), it's a good idea to put one or two spare blankets in a drawer, closet, or on a chair. Towels should be left in the guest room, if you do not have a guest bathroom. Other thoughtful touches are a box of tissues, light reading matter, a small bowl of fruit, glasses, and a jug of iced water placed beside the bed.

Guests invited for the weekend should be given some idea of clothes to bring, and if possible, informed of any special activities you plan for them—such as tennis, riding, fishing, or swimming. If you are going to entertain local friends or other weekenders in your home for cocktails or dinner and plan to dress up, mention this, too, so that women guests, in particular, know what to bring.

The entertainment you plan for your guests depends, of course, on your personal tastes and those of your guests. If you intend to make it a simple, relaxed weekend, with no specific activities other than swimming or walking, have a good supply of books, magazines, cards and other games, and records.

Always tell your guests the meal times, and if you plan something special for them let them know well in advance. They can be dressed to go out or meet other friends you have invited in for a party, and avoid a last minute scramble.

Remember that as a gracious hostess, you should never try to force rigid rules on your weekend guests, other than meal times and activities planned specially for them. Guests have been invited into your home to relax and enjoy themselves, and if they are too regimented they will feel uncomfortable. If they want to stay up late, listening to music, playing a card game, or chatting with other guests, they should be perfectly at liberty to do so. In this case, it is correct etiquette for you to go to bed and leave them to their own devices. The same rule applies to getting up in the morning. You can tell them the time breakfast is served, and suggest that if they want to sleep late they may have something light such as coffee and toast, or make breakfast for themselves. It is the same as entertaining in your home. Your guests are there to relax and enjoy themselves—etiquette should be used to help you accomplish this.

TABLE SETTINGS AND CENTERPIECES

A table set with special attention and care—one that is pretty and bright—makes dining with friends even more enjoyable. Pleasant surroundings and a relaxed atmosphere contribute to the relaxed mood of guests and to the success of your party, whether it's a semiformal dinner, a brunch buffet, or a luncheon. That pretty table is also a promise of more good things to come. It says that you've taken special care in preparing everything you have to serve and that your guests are going to be treated to the best you have.

A properly and prettily set table is a confidence builder for the hostess, too. She'll enjoy being the one to create the setting and knowing that she's delighting others, too.

What makes a pretty table? Think of what makes any work of art beautiful. It's a combination of color, scale, and proportion. An attractive color scheme will give the setting immediate eye appeal. Then, the table, the centerpiece, the large and small masses on the table should all be scaled to the size of the dining space and they should all be in good proportion to each other. If you're using candles, for example, their height should be compatible with the height of your glasses and your centerpiece.

Learning the art of combining colors and controlling scale and proportion in a table setting takes practice. Experience, again, is your best teacher. By browsing through china departments and looking through table setting books and magazines, you can begin your experience and assimilate some of the lessons taught. This chapter begins by showing you fundamentals—the correct ways to set a dinner table, a luncheon table, and buffet tables, then gives you ideas for centerpieces and novel table settings, and for unusual containers for centerpieces.

←**What could make** a setting say "springtime" more than a yellow-and-white breakfast on the patio? Daisy place mats pick up the theme set by the real daisies of the centerpiece. A refreshing touch, and the true color of spring, is provided by the green limes and leaves mounded into lemon yellow compotes.

TABLE SETTINGS

Half the fun of preparing a delicious meal lies in planning a pretty table setting as a background for serving. But it's important to remember that behind every table arrangement is one basic consideration—your family's and guest's convenience. Plan everything from the placement of the salad fork to the serving of the dessert with this and the rules of etiquette in mind.

The etiquette rules of table setting were designed with convenience in mind. Although in today's informal world the rules can often be broken, it is wise to know the correct methods of table setting for the different dining occasions to give you a plan to follow when the occasion demands.

The settings illustrated are for buffet service—both for an average-size group and for a crowd, for a semi-formal dinner, and for an informal luncheon. Each can be followed, adapted, or revised for your own specific needs.

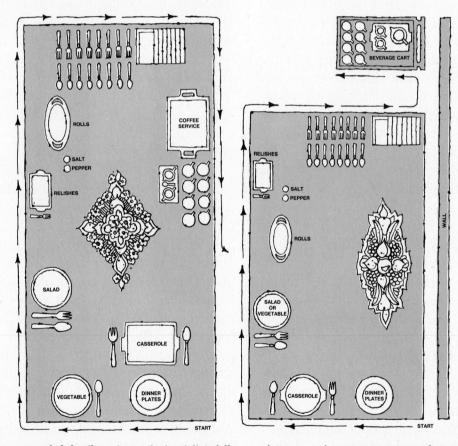

A successful buffet always looks delightfully easy to the guests—but as every hostess knows, it requires special planning. If space allows, place the buffet table in the middle of the room so guests can circulate around it. Or, you may choose to place the table just far enough away from the wall for the hostess to walk comfortably behind it. Use a cart or small table nearby for beverage. There is no hard-and-fast rule for setting a buffet, but it is important that guests can serve themselves in logical sequence. At one end of the table place the dinner plates and main dish. Place other foods such as salads, vegetable, buttered rolls, and relishes along with serving pieces near the edge of the table in easy reach. Leave enough room near each serving dish for guests to set their plates. Arrange silver and napkins so they can be picked up last, or set them on individual tables.

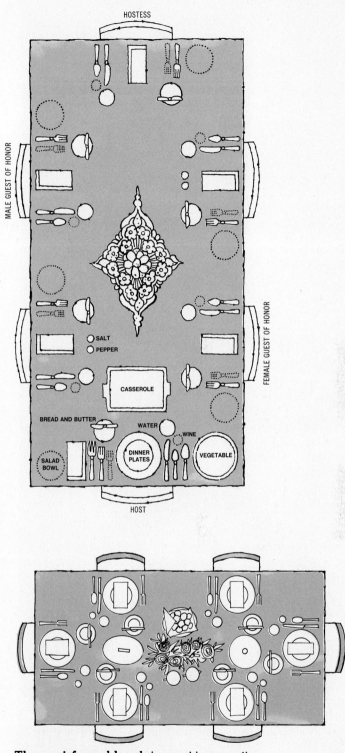

When serving English style, illustrated at the right, the setting is semi-formal. The main dishes are served at the table by the host. The host or hostess may serve the vegetables, then the plates are passed. In this service and in family-style service when everyone helps himself, the pieces indicated by the dotted lines are considered optional.

When the group is quite large, set twin arrangements of plates, food, silver, and napkins, on each side of the table. Guests form two lines helping themselves to the main dish, vegetable or salad, buttered rolls, relishes, and finally silver and napkins. If a sit-down buffet is possible, arrange small tables with silver, napkins, and glasses.

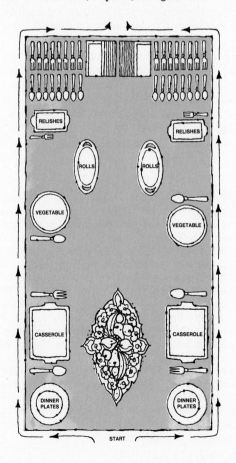

The semi-formal lunch is served just as a dinner. The only difference may be the number of courses offered—usually three at a lunch. The informal lunch table setting follows that of the informal dinner or the buffet. If the salad is served with the main course, it is placed to the left of the forks. The wine glass is optional.

The diagrams on the preceding pages illustrate the traditional way to set informal tables, semiformal tables, and buffet tables. The examples in the photographs add the extra note of design and color to the place settings showing tables actually ready for use.

The basic rules for correct dinner settings are, forks on the left, knives and spoons on the right, all placed from the outside in, in order of their use. Knife blade faces the plate. The napkin is placed beside the forks.

Place china and silver about one inch from the table edge and space settings about fifteen inches apart for the comfort and convenience of diners. Water glasses or goblets should be placed above the point of the knife; wine glasses go above the spoons.

For a luncheon setting follow the same rules as for dinner, however, use the smaller luncheon plate. If coffee is served, the cup and saucer should be placed just outside the top edge of the teaspoon. Two teaspoons should be set if the dessert served requires a spoon. Or the second spoon may be placed later on the dessert plate.

Buffet tables are not governed by hard and fast rules. Strive for attractive, artistic arrangement and one that progresses in logical order so guests find it easy to serve themselves. Place silverware at the end or on the tables so guests have fewer items to juggle.

Buffet suppers are a boon to the busy woman. The table is easy to set up and it requires much less "running-work" from the table to the kitchen than dinner. The buffet table is set up in a logical sequence. For a regular buffet, the plates, napkins, and silver are nearest the beginning. At a sit-down buffet, silver and napkins are placed on the individual tables. The main dish is next followed by the vegetables, rolls, condiments, and salad. Glasses are last unless already placed on tables, or on a separate, smaller table set up just for the beverages. A cart can be used for the dessert to be wheeled in after the dinner.

For a large buffet, use a table set out from the wall and set up identical services on both sides. For a smaller buffet, all you'll need is one side of a table set against the wall or a sideboard such as the one at the left. Be creative and artistic with your setting, but be practical, too.

A pretty, patio setting is perfect for an informal luncheon or midmorning brunch. Casual pottery helps set the mood, as does the informal buffet and table setting. Set the main course (individual casseroles hot from the oven or warming tray) on the table and use the same basic table setting plan that any lunch or dinner requires. But you can be more creative with the napkin design and silver placement. Use the buffet for the dessert table with everything set out ready for your guests to help themselves. By the time they've returned to your table, you've cleared it of the luncheon dishes and are ready to join your guests.

A special dinner requires the most traditional of table settings. Use your best china and silver, polished to glow, and follow the rules of etiquette. For a formal dinner, the bread plate is not used. For the semiformal dinner, shown here, it is optional. Place silver as you use it from the outside to the inside. Water glass goes above the knife, the wine glass to the right. As each course is completed, have the used plates and utensils removed. Bring in the dessert plates and spoons or forks separately at the end of the meal. It's a thoughtful way to pamper favorite guests.

TABLE-SETTING IDEAS

Ideas for your table settings and centerpieces are everywhere waiting for you to discover them. They can be inspired by your party theme, by your china or pottery, by your table linens, by the season of the year, or by an object in your home. The inspired creations in this chapter are an impetus to help you think of ideas of your own. For a beautifully and creatively set table is its own reward, and it helps put you into your best festive party mood.

Informal affairs call for care just as formal occasions do, so plan your table settings for both to fit the mood you want to establish.

Your casserole baking dishes (right) will have chameleon qualities when you change their purpose to flower containers. Place flowers in any trio of baking dishes at different heights, reserving the tallest flowers (tulips and willows here) for the back.

Awning-striped paper cups (lower right) hold bouquets of violets, cornflowers, and daisies. These do-it-yourself-in-minutes containers are made by gluing the hot drink cups together. To achieve different heights vary the number of cups in a stack.

Casual centerpiece containers (below) are laundry room treasures. For a bowl, slice the top from a gallon plastic bottle, then trim edges into points. Roll the points over a pencil. Paint both bottles and trim with raffia.

It's fun to discover pretty coordinates for your casual china. Let the color or pattern inspire you, then search through variety, import, and fabric shops for place mats and napkins. If you're a seamstress, you can sew your own.

The Persian inspired pottery (right) has an ornate overall pattern resembling transparent silk. It is combined with a saffron mat in a matching hue. The place-setting bouquet of amber chrysanthemums completes the monochromatic setting.

Casual table settings are appropriate for any informal occasion and they're fun to arrange as an impromptu surprise for your family dinner.

Creative silverware placement can add a touch of flair to the setting. The knife, fork, and spoon on the plate of daisies (below right) crisscross in contrast to the vertical stripes of the mat.

Daisies on the china inspired the boutonniere arrangement and the green background determined the color of the napkin. Color and pattern contrast is provided by the nubby, striped place mat.

Greek key pattern tracing the rim of this white china (below) can start a series of table-setting ideas. Here it is teamed with black, white, red, and blue for a Mediterranean country atmosphere. A pattern this austere would look equally at home on sophisticated shiny black or white mats or on a hot Mexican pink or turquoise. Napkins should contrast with the color of the place mats for a striking arrangement of opposites.

CENTERPIECE IDEAS

For an impromptu centerpiece (above) place a large candle on a footed gallery tray. This one is trimmed with wax limes and has its own stand. Simple candles without their own stands are just as interesting and can be elevated on a plate and surrounded with a luscious assortment of seasonal fruit or vegetables.

Candles anytime—they'll change an ordinary meal to a banquet. Novelty candles such as the ones above come in many distinctive designs. The primitive Egyptian allure of this setting is echoed by using ordinary building bricks (with ready-made holes) sprayed black and an inexpensive plaster statue. Completing the Nile scene is the place mat, sprayed black to fit the scheme.

Fragrant roses (right) and candles that won't burn away add the elegance to this setting. The combination of butane gas candles and a handful of garden blooms is arranged in a low rectangular bowl. To achieve the asymmetrical effect, elevate one candle on a pinholder. Low stands which accompany these candles can be removed to vary the heights. Try combining candles with fruit foliage, or with a figurine for a variety of moods.

Wedding tables deserve memorable treatment, no matter how simple or elaborate your plans may be. A candle sconce, usually hanging from the ceiling, has chain and bracket removed for this dramatic centerpiece. A bowl inside the ironwork holds mums, snapdragons, and transitional greens (those in season). Place all on an elegant gold and white cloth for an opulent effect.

For a quaint and courtly look on informal tables at home, add fresh flowers to oversize champagne-sherbets (available at department or variety stores). You can buy glasses with ready-made raffia wrappings on the stems—or trim plain ones yourself. Average-size sherbets filled with similar bouquets make ideal card-table and guest-book table centerpieces for a reception.

An airy, floating centerpiece is ideal for the main wedding party table. Select any long glass or silver tray and secure a custard cup with posy putty a little off center. Arrange towering stems of acacia with a few carnations at the base. Add glass bubbles and tiny bird figurines at the base. Use small glass bowls for miniatures elsewhere.

A duplicate of the bride's bouquet becomes the centerpiece. Order a small double of the bouquet, and the bridesmaid's, too, if the table is extra long. Spray one or more shell baskets gold or silver and attach the bouquets with florist's wire. For height, tip the baskets at the back with plastic foam. Add a boutonniere at each place setting.

The rules of placement and arrangement of centerpieces were at one time very rigid and strictly observed. Today, although there are still a few rules of etiquette applying to height, type, and placement, the rigid standards have been relaxed and the hostess is allowed to use her ingenuity.

The few regulations that do apply today are common courtesies. No centerpiece should be so tall or large that guests must strain to talk to the person across from them. Candles, too, should be easy to see over or around. They should be either above or below eye level, and, if used, they must be lighted.

The formal dinner is the only time when a centerpiece standard is a must. The arrangement, usually floral, is placed in the center of the table and candles are always used. You can still, however, use your ingenuity in the arrangement and the materials you use.

For all other meals let your imagination run. Materials can be whatever you have on hand or whatever you find. Just be sure they're appropriate to the table and occasion. Dried or fresh flowers are always favorites and can be arranged in countless ways. Fresh fruit,

polished and shiny, is practical as well as decorative. Even garden vegetables can be arranged into clever and colorful table-piece designs.

You can make tin can flowers, paper cutouts, paper-mache fruit, and fancy candies yourself. For holidays your centerpiece can be the motif of the day—blown eggs for Easter, gaily wrapped packages at Christmas, a horn of plenty at Thanksgiving, or miniature flags and firecrackers for the Fourth of July.

Porcelain figurines and ceramic creations make elegant centerpieces for semi-formal occasions. Family heirlooms can dress up any table.

Nor are you limited in your choice of containers. Within the limits of good design and color principles, you can choose from a multitude of styles. Vegetable dishes to match your china or pottery, ceramic bowls and mugs, silver tureens, goblets, kitchen pots and pans, colanders, and woven baskets can hold an assortment of centerpiece materials. Visit variety stores, antique shops, gift shops, and department stores to build up your collection of containers. Do remember to keep the shape and style of your table in mind.

A backyard picnic centerpiece is composed of cutout gentian from four paper plates. They're wired to stand at uneven heights in a footed brass bowl and surrounded with sprigs of fresh huckleberry. Cover wire stems with floral tape.

Cutouts, this time of pseudo-sunflowers, are from colorful paper place mats. Some of the circles are rolled to simulate buds. Leaves are cut from four thicknesses of bittergreen paper napkins. Flowers may be glued back to back and grouped in a berry box.

Japanese lanterns are simple and effective. Cut the birds and geometric designs (they resemble lanterns) from paper plates and hang them on a graceful branch that's been stripped of its bark. Wire the birds upright and hang the lanterns.

Fill the glasses—does your cupboard shelter the remnants of broken sets of glassware? These stray pieces can be combined to achieve effective floral centerpieces—and the more casually arranged, the more exciting the results.

Inexpensive glass bowls and one tall tumbler are grouped on a small oval tray. Add a dramatic touch with smooth-textured leaves fixed at right angles to clusters of vivid carnations. The stems, showing through the glasses, add to the charm.

Three towers of long-stemmed black glasses are stacked at different heights, giving a wholly contemporary feeling. Each skyscraper holds its own individual casual bouquet of garden-picked bright pink roses. You can spray paint clear glass in velvety black or in colors to match your flowers if you don't already have the right hue.

By fitting goblets base to base like these, or elevating like-size tumblers on stands and by combining squat ice-cream dishes in duets you can create unusual silhouettes. Even bowls and pitchers, large or small, serve well for flower containers.

Quaint with the charm of a country kitchen, this pressed-glass cream and sugar shows off a quantity of tiny mums, scaled correctly to the size of the containers. Mass the flowers at the base for a low line and place tall stems at an angle. The stand for the pitcher is used to break like heights.

Your kitchen cupboards should be a storehouse of containers for centerpieces. You can mound fresh fruit in vegetable bowls, arrange lengths of garden vegetables and gourds on serving platters, pile dainty glass balls and bibelots in a silver bread server, and float single blossoms in cups.

ETIQUETTE

One of the most enjoyable assets of a home is being able to invite your friends to share it with you.

This act of sharing has many rewards. You derive pleasure from giving your guests pleasure, and in seeing them truly at ease in your home. There is satisfaction in knowing that your friends appreciate the comfort and atmosphere you have created; and also appreciate your talents as a good hostess.

You can be a successful hostess. It does not require any formal kind of training or an academic degree, but thoughtfulness, caring about your guests and wanting to make them happy. You do this by putting the comfort and well-being of your guests first and observing the rules of etiquette. This is the core from which everything else flows, and it ensures the ultimate success of your entertaining on all of its levels. Of course, we can't be perfect hostesses overnight. There are countless things which must be included. It is also quite obvious that the woman who has had some experience is going to be a little more adept at entertaining than the beginner. She will have learned through trial and error. The beginner is bound to be more nervous, even apprehensive, simply through lack of this experience.

But the beginner can lessen her apprehension. With planning, thinking, and knowing a few simple rules, even the novice can give a wonderful party (be it large or small) and make it a success. And can enjoy herself as well.

Etiquette in entertaining is vital. It can make or break the hostess and the occasion. Of course, literally speaking, etiquette means good manners and good manners means consideration for another person— so again we come back to thoughtfulness and the hostess' relationship to her guests.

←**A beautifully appointed table** and a sparkling clean house let guests know that they are truly welcome. The little extra attentions that shows the hostess cares are what make us feel at home and at ease. Who wouldn't feel festive and welcomed in a setting as lovely as the one pictured.

Lunch
Monday, April 3 - 1:15

Mrs. John Morton

R.S.V.P.   1617 Spanish Lane

Dinner
Saturday, January 6, 8 p.m.

Mrs. Robert Bradford

2 E. 86 Street

R.S.V.P.

Dinner
Tuesday, May 10, 8 p.m.

Mrs. Wayne Byal

R.S.V.P.   700 Park Avenue

Cocktails - Monday,
March 15, 6-8

Mrs. Eric Lee Sage

9 Walley Road

Your hostess-relationship with guests begins the very moment you decide to entertain. It is then you will determine which friends to invite, those who are compatible and will mix well together, and those who will enjoy the type of party you are planning. After all, inviting the appropriate guests to the right kind of party is important for the success of your party and for the pleasure of those you invite. Some people dislike cocktail parties, and are much happier at smaller, more intimate gatherings. It is poor etiquette to invite them to a cocktail party. So making sure that both your guests and the occasion are congenial is your first act of consideration and the right step in ensuring your success as a hostess.

This consideration must continue through all the progressive stages of your planning—from your choice of food and beverages, eating time, and type of entertainment, if any, to mode of dress for the occasion. Remember always that you are inviting friends to your home to relax and to enjoy themselves, so all of the little things which will please them must be your primary considerations.

Invitations

Inviting your guests is the next step. You, as the hostess, are the one to extend the invitation just as you reply to all you receive. And you address them to those you want to invite. To families, include names of both adults (as Mr. and Mrs.) and of the children and to singles, including their title (Miss, Mr.).

Since some of the more rigid rules of the etiquette of extending invitations have been relaxed, many women find themselves a little confused about the correct form of sending requests. Today, the simplest way to determine this is to divide entertaining into two categories, i.e. informal/semiformal and formal. The type of entertaining you are planning and the degree of formality decides the mode of invitation you should use.

Informal/semiformal

Invitations to informal or semiformal dinner parties, luncheons, teas, cocktails, buffets, children's or teen-age parties can be extended by visiting cards, informals, personal notes, preprinted invitations, or telephone.

The telephone is permissible today and is the most popular form of issuing invitations for informal occasions. But when telephoning an invitation, do make sure that you state quite clearly the date, time, and type of party you are giving. Whenever possible, it's best to give the recipient a few days notice, preferably a week.

If you take the trouble to suggest the kind of dress your guests should wear, your prestige as a considerate and courteous hostess will increase. This avoids the necessity for guests to phone for advice the day before the party, when you're busy with preparations, or face the embarrassment of arriving in the wrong clothes.

When you are inviting friends from out of town to an informal party, it is better to send a written invitation. Written invitations are also sent out for house parties or weekend parties, and to your weekend guests, however informally you intend to entertain them.

But the choice is yours. If you do prefer sending invitations through the mail for informal/semiformal events, you can choose between the other forms mentioned earlier.

Visiting cards

Today, the visiting card, in a matching envelope, has become quite popular as a mode of extending invitations to informal parties in place of the written note. The cards vary in size, but are usually about 2 by 3 inches. The post office will not accept very small envelopes (the minimum size is 3 by 4½ inches), so it is wise to order a more practical size of envelope. The envelope will be larger than the card unless you order larger size cards to fit.

On the visiting card carrying an invitation, you can draw a line through the engraved name, if you intend to sign your first name to the invitation. But this is optional and a matter of personal preference. The letters R.S.V.P. (or R.s.v.p.) should be written in the bottom left hand corner.

The samples of visiting cards on page 134 illustrate the different elements that can be included in the engraving and handwriting.

Informals

The small fold-over cards, known as informals, are ideal for extending informal invitations. Many women prefer their less businesslike nature to visiting cards. White, off white, or brightly colored ones are available at all stationers and you can use them as they are or have them engraved with your name (across the center) or your monogram (in the upper left corner).

On the brightly colored informals (not strictly correct for semiformal affairs) you can use a vivid, contrasting color for the monogram, and use brightly colored felt-tipped pens coordinated with the color of the paper for handwriting the invitations. If you do a lot of entertaining or have many occasions to write brief notes to friends, it is worth investing in the multipurpose monogrammed informals.

It's just a little nicer to send out hand-written rather than typewritten notes no matter how casual your party. Of course, for semiformal occasions the typewriter is never correct.

Personal notes

Plain writing paper designed as a single sheet is an acceptable medium for issuing invitations. Personal writing paper is available monogrammed, engraved, bordered, or plain. Be sure to purchase matching envelopes and include full name and address if not on the paper.

Preprinted invitations

If informals of the kind mentioned do not appeal to you, you can buy a variety of attractively printed cards designed as invitations for cocktail parties, buffets, informal dinners, and children's parties.

But remember, when writing an invitation on an unmarked or unmonogrammed informal, to include your full name. It is wise to include the address, too. Informal written invitations should be mailed at least ten days in advance of the party date.

Formal

Formal invitations are sent out on various occasions—the formal dinner, the formal dance, the debut, the official luncheon or reception, and, of course, the wedding and reception.

Formal invitations are engraved, or hand-written (never printed) on conservative white or off-white paper, in the third-person, and are sent out two weeks ahead of time. For some occasions, such as the wedding when guests may be coming in from other towns, they may be mailed three to four weeks ahead.

The engraved invitation comes in two forms, either with the entire message engraved, or with parts engraved and the rest left open to be filled in by hand. Both are perfectly correct and the choice depends on personal preference.

The fill-in card is also white or off-white. Use black ink to write the fill-in information, never a bright color ink or a typewritten message.

Formal handwritten invitations

If you do not want to have formal invitations engraved, you can use any personal formal writing paper, always white or off-white since this is the correct form, and handwrite them. The third-person is used, as in all formal invitations, and if the stationery is not engraved with the address, this is given at the bottom under the time. Examples of the engraved formal invitation, handwritten formal invitation, formal fill-in invitation, and informal monogrammed paper invitation are illustrated below.

Mr. and Mrs. Arthur Riser
request the pleasure of your company
at dinner
on Thursday, August the sixth
at eight o'clock
4500 Park Lane
R.S.V.P.

Mr. and Mrs. Robert Bradford request the pleasure of Mr. and Mrs. Garman's company at dinner on Wednesday, August the ninth at eight o'clock
R.S.V.P.   2 East Eighty-sixth Street

Mr. and Mrs. Dwaine Francis
request the pleasure of
Mr. and Mrs. Annau's
company at dinner
on Wednesday, the Fifth of June
29 Highland Avenue
R.S.V.P. at eight o'clock

BB
May 10th
Dear Joyce,
Could you and Dennis join us for a buffet supper on Saturday, May 17th at 8 p.m.?
12 Park Lane   Brenda Brooke

PLANNING FOR PERFECTION

We all know that it's the little things that count—little details which add up to make the total picture, and which ensure or mar the success of a party. As a hostess, there are many tiny things you can do to add to the general comfort of your guests, and most of them can be done in advance of the party, some even a few days before.

Smokers

You can set your extra ashtrays out before the party—the day before, if you will not be using the party room until then. Always have plenty of them around, for apart from guaranteeing protection to your soft and hard furnishings, they help to make your guests feel at ease. There is nothing more discomforting to a smoker than a room without an ashtray. Be sure, too, that your ashtrays are a good size and comfortably spaced throughout the room.

Have the ashtrays emptied at regular intervals. Don't try stacking up several little ashtrays; this deprives your guests and is awkward for you to handle. Instead use a silent butler to hold ash and cigarette ends, or a large ashtray, into which you can empty the smaller ones. A thoughtful hostess puts out filter and non-filter cigarettes in several convenient places.

Smoke problems

If you know that most of your guests smoke, it's a good idea to have several lighted candles around the room. In some mysterious way they help to clear the atmosphere of smoke. You can buy specially treated candles at most variety stores today which do this little job even more effectively. They come in multicolored glass containers and add to the overall decorative effect in the room as well as serve a useful purpose. Most important, they ensure comfort for nonsmokers.

Napkins

If you are serving snacks with cocktails, it is advisable to have plenty of napkins around. It's wise to have small stacks of them placed in strategic spots around the room. Often it's a good idea to offer guests a small linen napkin to begin with, and then let them help themselves from the reinforcement stacks of paper ones. But it is quite correct to use paper napkins only.

Snacks

Nuts, chips, crackers, and other crisp foods can be put in dishes and placed in the room several hours before the party. Dips and more perishable snacks can be prepared the day before and kept in the refrigerator until you need them (good time-savers). Again make sure they are conveniently placed, and are within easy reach of every guest.

Coaster-trays

Manipulating a glass, a snack, a napkin, often a cigarette, and trying to shake hands presents awkward problems to everyone, more so to female guests who are usually carrying pocketbooks as well. It is quite correct today, particularly at large cocktail parties, not to shake hands but to acknowledge the introduction with a smile and a nod of the head. Even so, this still does not altogether remove the problem of dealing with a handful of food and drink.

One way to solve this difficulty is to provide your guests with spacious coaster-trays that will hold both drinks and snacks and which can be easily held in one hand. You might buy sets of the inexpensive Indian papier-mache type; small wooden plates from Scandinavia, or even provide small tin trays with a brightly colored Chinese-lacquer finish. Alternatively, you could use almost any kind of small, attractive plate or

Snack trays, roomy enough to hold both the snacks and a drink, are welcomed by guests who don't want to be juggling experts at a party.

Convenience is a main feature to look for when selecting trays. Divided plates with a special indentation for glasses are easiest to handle.

Other qualities to look for include a nonskid surface, a rim around the plate, ease in handling, and, of course, an attractive appearance.

miniature tray, provided it is easy to hold in one hand, has plenty of room for a glass and the snacks, and does not have a slippery surface.

The coaster trays protect your furniture surfaces, and provide extra comfort for your guests.

Beauty tray

For that special party touch prepare a pretty beauty tray for your guest bath. The items on the tray need not be elaborate—they can be as simple as a new comb, a pretty box of facial tissues, a light cologne, and a can of hair spray. Place the tray in a prominent and convenient place. It's a nice gesture and a welcome one to those who may have forgotten one of the items of their own. The consideration will give you the stamp of a "super" hostess. Naturally, fresh soap and towels should also be provided. This task can be scheduled and accomplished early in the party day.

Hopefully, if all the stages of your planning have worked on schedule, you will have time for a rest before getting dressed for the party. Even if it is for only fifteen minutes, put your feet up and relax. It will refresh you and put you in a party frame of mind.

Greeting guests

First impressions linger for a long time, and the way you greet your guests will help to determine the mood of the party. Occasionally a hostess may unintentionally be rude, offhand, or cool simply because she is exhausted or worried because she has forgotten a last-minute item. To avoid giving guests the unwelcome feeling, check your planning lists well in advance of guest arrival times and make sure you and the host are refreshed, ready, and waiting in the living or party room ten minutes before guests are due.

You and the host should greet the

guests together. Then, if you have no help, and if the party is small, the host hangs the coats and wraps in a hall closet. If there are more coats than the closet can hold, it is common practice to hang only the men's coats in the hall. Women guests are shown to a bedroom and asked to place their coats on the bed. This arrangement is convenient for you and for the women guests who then have a chance for last-minute makeup repairs. If you do have help, then the helper takes the coats.

Once you have greeted your guests, and dispensed with coats, you and the host take the guests to the party room. While the host fixes the drinks of their choice, you introduce the latest arrivals to the other guests. If the party is small, take each guest around to meet everyone else; but if it's a large party, introduce the newcomers to two or three people, then let them circulate alone. You can safely assume that most people will introduce themselves to other guests, but do keep an eye on a guest who knows no one and is a little shy.

If, after greeting guests at the door, more arrive immediately, either you or the host should look after the first arrivals while the other stays to greet the newcomers. In fact, one of you should always stay within sight of the front door to greet guests. And both of you should avoid being out of the room at the same time while the party is in progress.

When you have no help, your host acts as bartender during the party and you act as waitress. If serving becomes too hectic, the host can ask a close male friend to assist him with the drinks and you may ask a friend to pass around snacks. The latter can be avoided if you place trays of snacks around the room. A friend may help you replenish trays in the kitchen as the food runs out and pass them around.

Conversation

Once your guests have all arrived and are settled with drinks and snacks, you can move from group to group (if it's a large party) making sure everyone is comfortable and has what he wants. The host should also circulate so that your guests have an opportunity to chat with both of you. If you have a small group of six or eight guests for dinner it will be easy to sit with them during cocktails and join in the conversation. Trips to the kitchen should be as brief as you can possibly make them.

Keeping the conversation going is always the duty of the host and hostess. If you are an adept and relaxed hostess, this is not difficult. You will already have invited friends who have some threads of mutual interest to the party—it makes your task of keeping the chatter alive so much easier. But even among old friends, it's wise to have some new "openers" so you can add stimulating ideas to the conversation, then let your guests carry on themselves.

To make a conversation-party interesting, try to develop a skill in bringing out your guests. You can do this easily if you know their interests and hobbies well beforehand. Once you know what intrigues them, you can lead the talk around to those subjects. To those interested in theater, you can mention a new play and encourage them to tell what they know about it—the same with books, movies, music, gardening, gourmet cooking, and travel. Or you might mention something you have read in a newspaper or magazine on a subject you know will interest them.

As a hostess, the bane of your life, and the party, is the guest who falls into total silence and almost refuses to be brought into the conversation. It might be that such a person feels shy, tired, or simply disinterested in what the others are talking about. It might be that he just enjoys listening to others. In any event, don't try to force him into the conversation. Let him continue to listen quietly and you will probably find that he makes an interesting contribution later when another subject is brought up with which he feels more confident and interested.

But never try too hard to get your party going. If you are relaxed and let things take their natural course, your guests will relax, too. They will get acquainted with each other and both general and group conversation will develop quite naturally. You do not need to feel that you must provide all the conversation. If necessary, you can turn the conversation to other subjects, particularly if you feel that guests are getting into controversial subjects that could lead to heated discussions and ill feelings. But this does not mean you have to hold the conversation.

Eating Times

As the hostess, you have a certain amount of leeway when it comes to choosing the time for meals. Although this is very much a personal preference on your part, it is wiser to stay within the times of local customs.

Eating times vary across the country, but most of them stay more or less within the time schedules listed below.

Brunch: Between 10:30 a.m. and 1 p.m.

Luncheon: Usually 12:30 or 1 p.m.

Buffet luncheon: Usually starts at 12:30 and is served until 2 p.m.

Dinner: Usually 8 p.m. in large metropolitan areas; as early as 6:30 and 7 p.m. in the West and Midwest. Guests are usually invited thirty or forty-five minutes before dinner, for drinks.

Buffet suppers: Usually at 8:30 or 9 p.m. For special occasion parties they can be served later, but guests should be so informed.

Coffee parties: Usually between 10 a.m. and noon.

Tea parties: Usually 4 p.m.; never any later than 4:30 p.m.

Cocktail parties: Usually from 5 p.m. until 7 p.m. although personal preference can dictate the hours. For instance, in large cities where people are often working until 5:30 p.m. hostesses prefer to make cocktails from 6 p.m. to 8 p.m.

Seating Arrangements

Seating arrangements, which at first may seem baffling, are actually relatively simple and follow a set pattern.

The seating at the formal luncheon, the formal dinner, and the informal dinner are all the same. You, as the hostess, sit at one end of the table and your husband, as the host, sits at the opposite end. It is preferable that you sit at the end of the table near the kitchen door, or close to the door through which the help brings the food.

If you have an honored guest, he or she is placed either to the right of you or of your husband. The dinner partner of the guest of honor sits at the opposite end of the table, also on the right. For example, if the honored guest is a woman, she will sit to the right of the host and her dinner partner will be on the hostess's right. If the guest of honor is a man, he will sit to the right of the hostess and his dinner partner will sit on the right of the host. The second most important male guest will sit on the hostess's left and the second most important female guest on the host's left.

If however, you have no guest of honor, seating is left to your personal preference. Usually a person of seniority or a guest you see infrequently is given a place of honor on the right of you or your husband, depending on whether it's a man or a woman.

The other guests are seated as you wish to place them around the table, alternating the men and the women. If you happen to have more men than women, or more women than men, try to distribute the sexes as evenly as possible without making it obvious.

Buffet dinners and suppers

You can seat your guests in two ways at a buffet dinner or supper. The choice depends on preference and space.

If your buffet is set up in the dining room or any room other than the party room, guests may help themselves to the food and return to the party room where you will have allocated plenty of chairs. Guests can balance their plates in their laps to eat. However, your guests will be much more comfortable and you will avoid spills and accidents if you put a small table (the folding type) next to each chair. There are many styles available ranging from the inexpensive, but attractive, to the very costly and elegant that will adapt to the style of your furnishings. Alternatively, you can make sure that each guest's chair is within easy reach of a coffee table or an end table.

A second way of seating guests at a buffet is to set out a number of small tables, to accommodate four to six guests, and chairs. These can be set up anywhere that there is room for them. This arrangement will depend on the amount of space you have, but it is the most comfortable for all. The tables should have cheerful cloths and should be set with silver, napkins, and pepper and salt as at an informal dinner. The guests help themselves to the food at the buffet and return to find a seat at one of the tables. If you wish, you can direct them to tables, mixing your guests as you think fit. As a gracious hostess you should keep visiting each table between courses to see that your guests have everything they need.

Seating arrangements at breakfast, brunch, luncheon, tea, and children's parties are very flexible and they can be as relaxed and as informal as you wish to make them.

Tell your guests what to wear

Friends really appreciate—and applaud —the hostess who is thoughtful enough to give them an idea of what clothes are appropriate to wear to the party.

Yet all too often the area of party apparel is overlooked and the would-be guests are left in a state of quandary about how to dress for the occasion, particularly when there is a choice.

If you are telephoning your invitations, it's easy enough, and certainly courteous, to give some idea of what to wear. The most polite way of doing this is to tell your female guests what you are going to wear; if she is going to be accompanied by a male friend or her husband, you should also tell her what your husband will be wearing.

When the party you are giving is informal and you suggest casual clothes, it's best to clarify your approach to "casual." If the informal party is a barbecue or a buffet to be held out of doors, and you intend to wear either pants or patio pajamas, then mention your plans.

In this way, the guest is in no doubt about what you actually intend the party to be. You can also add that she can wear the same type of outfit if she pleases. If your husband plans to wear sports clothes—slacks, a sweater, and light jacket, you can mention his plans, too, so that her husband will be saved the embarrassment or discomfort of arriving in a dark suit and tie.

If, on the other hand, you are giving an informal dinner with a degree of formality to it, don't confuse your guest by saying it's informal and leaving it at that. Explain that it is going to be a little more dressy and tell her what you intend to wear. By being specific about your party dress plans, no matter what the occasion, you save your guests any worry and the trouble of having to call you later to inquire.

With written invitations you can also add a line about clothes, although these invitations are often self-explanatory. A beach party means beach clothes, but you could add a line suggesting guests bring suits if you do not intend for them to arrive in bathing attire.

Invitations to cocktails can be a trifle confusing. If the card categorically states *cocktail party*, then your guests know it will be slightly more dressy than just an invitation to *cocktails*. If you are not giving a large party and just inviting friends over for drinks, you can write the word *informal* at the bottom of the cocktail invitation.

On invitations to a *very formal dinner, formal dinner-dance, formal birthday party/dinner, formal anniversary party/dinner* it is correct etiquette to write *black tie* on the bottom, if the invitation is not engraved, or if you are handwriting formal invitations. This leaves the woman guest in no doubt about her clothes. She'll check her wardrobe for her prettiest formal.

When giving special-occasion parties, and when you intend guests to come in clothes depicting the theme of your party (Halloween, St. Valentine's Day, etc.) then write *fancy dress* on the invitation. Weekend guests should be informed of what clothes to bring, particularly if you will be engaging in sports activities.

Multiple hostessing

There are many occasions when you might want to give a joint party with a friend, when both of you would be hostesses. The party could be a shower for a bride-to-be or a mother-to-be, an all-girl engagement party for a bride-to-be, a joint children's or teen-age party, a buffet supper for the local ladies club, or a luncheon for a new arrival in your community. The rules for multiple hostessing are simple and quite specific.

(a) You *jointly* decide in whose home the party is to be held or, if on the outside, where.

(b) Together you talk over and make all the plans. They must be *satisfactory to both of you.*

(c) You prepare a *mutual guest list* and *share* the burden of writing out the invitations, or telephoning the invitations.

(d) You send out invitations in *both your names*—but do be sure you include the address where the party is to be held.

(e) You *share* all costs equally.

(f) All chores, such as marketing, cooking, preparations, and decorations, even entertaining, are *shared equally.*

(g) You greet guests *together*, as husband-wife hosts would, and you both act as full-time hostesses all evening.

This is the correct, and also the fairest way of dividing the duties and responsibilities of multiple hostessing. If one of the hostesses has a preference she can take care of a certain chore. For instance, one may prefer to do all the marketing or all the cooking. But again, allocation of chores must be fair.

The late-staying guest

Perhaps the biggest bane of every hostess's life is the late-staying guest. This is the "sitter" who wants another drink or simply wants to talk, when everyone else want to call it a day. There are several hints you can drop, but they must be dropped delicately.

You and your husband can pointedly not join them in that "last" drink. If this doesn't work, you can start clearing away empty glasses and ashtrays and tidying the room. Alternatively, you can say, in a nice way, that your husband has to get up very early and must be excused. This technique usually works, where all the others fail. There is one unbreakable rule, however, and that is that you as the hostess, must stay until the bitter end, even though your husband can be excused.

Saying good-bye to guests

When it's time for your guests to leave, your husband gets their coats if they are in a hall closet, and you accompany women guests to the bedroom if their coats have been placed there. Your husband helps the departing guests on with their coats, then either the host or hostess sees the guests to the door. But do not close your door until the guests are on their way by foot or by car. And, if you live in an apartment house, you or your husband take the departing guests to the elevator and see them into it. In the case of unaccompanied women guests, the host sees them into a taxi. As a hostess, you are responsible for the comfort and well-being of your guests the moment they arrive until they are on their way home.

Guest Etiquette

Every hostess is also a guest at some time. Her experience as a hostess will make her a better guest because she knows what she wants, likes, and expects from the visitors in her home. There are a few do's and don'ts that the novice as well as the experienced guest should remember.

The first time the invited guest is asked to know the rules of courtesy is when he receives an invitation to a social gathering. It's most courteous to reply immediately to the invitation following the form in which the invitation was given—a telephone reply to a telephone request, a handwritten note to a handwritten note.

The next courtesy is promptness both

in arriving and departing. The ideal guest arrives on or a few minutes after the appointed hour (and only a few minutes) and does not linger and linger after the other guests have departed.

Every hostess welcomes and invites often those who contribute to the party —in conversation, in cooperation when asked to join in, in lending a helping hand inconspicuously. The guest does not need to take over the evening as the "life of the party" or become a third host and assume the role of the party-giver, he just needs to be an active participant and help make the party a success.

Moderation is a good rule for a guest to follow—in the eating, drinking, and the merrymaking.

Every party requires some kind of a thank you. It's possible to thank the host and hostess at the door, with a phone call, or with a note, but some form is necessary.

When leaving a party, the guest should not circulate in his overcoat saying good-bye to others. The others may not want to leave just yet, but may feel pushed to do so.

It's always nice to return hospitality although it's not necessary to plan an event just like the original one. Even the bachelor should make some attempt to repay the host and hostess.

The most important thing to remember, and that thing encompasses all else, is to be the guest you'd like to have if you were the party's hostess.

A gift for your hostess

When to send or take a little gift to your hostess depends very much on the occasion and, of course, upon your relationship with her.

If, after a dinner or party, you wish to show your appreciation and say "thank you" in a more substantial way than sending a note, you can send flowers with a brief message on a card. Correct etiquette is to send the flowers *after* the dinner or party. Some people send them on the morning of the day the party or dinner is given. It is a nice gesture, but inconvenient to the hostess: she will have planned her flower arrangements already and may not have a place for the extras. For the same reason, you should *never* take flowers with you. The hostess will undoubtedly have her hands full with last minute preparations and other guests, when you arrive. You can send a bouquet of flowers the evening before the day of the dinner—this is permissible, although not strictly correct either.

The important thing is that you let the hostess know that you enjoyed yourself. A telephone call followed by a note of thanks is often more touching for the hostess than the receipt of an expensive gift.

It is not necessary, but it is always courteous to take your weekend hostess a small gift—or alternatively something for her children. If you do not know her too well, an expensive gift will only embarrass her, so pick out a present that is not too costly. Appropriate little gifts include items such as a gift box of fancy soaps, an unusual plant, a selection of novelty cheeses, a collection of colorful matches and several amusing ashtrays, or a fun cook book. The gifts are generally something for the house and are never so costly that they seem like a payment. If you know your hostess's tastes well, you could take a book or record you know she will enjoy and doesn't have, a box of her favorite candy, perfume, or a set of felt-tipped pens and colorful stationery. You can send a gift after the weekend too—either way is correct. For children in the family, a small, quiet toy or something for them to eat would be sufficient.

Again, a note of thanks is necessary, and any gift should delight the hostess and not embarrass her.

The gift you take for Christmas, birthdays, and anniversaries will depend on the closeness of your relationship with your hostess. Obviously if she is an old and dear friend, you will take a fairly substantial gift. If, on the other hand, you do not know her too well, it is best to take something small and amusing. Should you be at a loss to know what to give for a specific anniversary, most department stores will make constructive suggestions.

PARTY GAMES

If you're planning a game-playing party, you have an almost endless selection of games from which to choose. There are the always-popular favorites such as Charades, Twenty Questions, Categories, and Anagrams that require little or no special equipment and can be played almost anywhere at any time. Other favorites—Monopoly, Clue, Scrabble, Checkers, and Chess do need the game boards and playing pieces, but all are easily obtained and are excellent for a party.

New game editions are better than ever—some are variations of the old favorites and some are entirely new. Some are action and some are quiet, some are concentration games, some are wit games, some are word games, some are manual dexterity games, some are even games designed for children that appeal to adults as well. You'll be able to find a game geared to every taste and age.

When the majority of your guests are game aficionados they'll need little persuasion to join in the new or old games. But if you've never introduced these party pepper-uppers before, here are a few tips you will want to know. Don't try to inveigle the entire group into the game. Let the eager ones take over and draw the shy ones into the action. Concentrate on games that take no more than five minutes to explain. Do watch out for signs of boredom and be ready with a substitution or a signal to halt. If you have a wide game selection, gear your choice of games to the mood and particular interests of your guests.

This chapter is designed primarily to let you know what is available in party games, both the new editions and the old ones. It also tells you which are appropriate for the quiet and the active times. From this listing, you'll be able to select just the games you'll need.

←**Your steady hand** and balancing skill keep the little acrobat on his unsteady perch in the game of Tip-it. Lively games as this keep the party moving at amazing speed. Hours will seem like minutes and you may end up serving breakfast to your happy game-players.

*Choose party games
to fit the mood of
your guests*

Parlor games are staging a big revival and the new editions are better than ever. Some require guile and concentration, others manual dexterity, still others a way with words. This game, a variation of the popular Scrabble, is called Twin Scribbage. It's a fast word game that requires each player to complete his turn at creating a word before the sand slips through the timer. Since it calls for fast action, the game will keep your party moving —to the delight of all present.

Raucous games for lively evenings demand dexterity and nerves of steel. In the center is "Hoopla," a game of skill and balance. This little acrobat spins around on a track and spears a plastic circle during each revolution. "Kaboom" is another cliffhanger that will keep you waiting for the pump that finally breaks the balloon. The number of pumps you're allowed depends on the number you spin. At the right is "Bowl-A-Strike," a bowling alley complete with tenpins, ball, and scorekeeper.

Where you play the game is as important as when or what you play. Be sure there's adequate room for refreshments, game boards, and other necessary accessories. This drum table was called into use to hold the party game and the home office desk became the buffet and snack table.

The game is Tiddly Cardwinks, a sophisticated version of Tiddly Winks. It lets you play your favorite card game by flipping the "winks" into the three-dimensional plastic playing field.

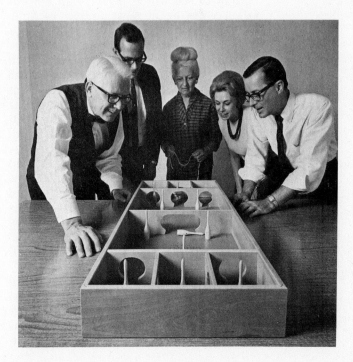

When you plan your party of games, you'll need to consider the mood and particular interests of your guests. For "Skittles" you'll want a group that enjoys lively activity. Small tenpins are set up in a series of compartments in a "Skittles" playing field. Players spin tops from a hole in the front of the box and try to bowl over the pins. It's a great after-dinner entertainment and it can be played by a number of people in teams—or, for smaller party gatherings, individually.

PARTY GAME SELECTIONS

Party games can be divided into several categories. These four are representative of the many types available and several games are listed under each. Since it is impossible to explain the rules of each in detail in the limited space, additional reference material is listed in the bibliography on page 192.

Team games or parlor games

Charades has been a popular party game for many years. One way to play the game is to divide your guests into two teams. Give each team from five to ten slips of paper, each with a word or phrase written on it. One player from each team reads one of the slips of paper, then must act out in pantomime in front of his team members what the paper says. The first team to guess correctly all of the words or phrases is the winner. The phrases may be song or book titles, popular quotations, advertising slogans, or any category you choose.

The game can also be played with individuals pantomiming before the entire group to see which person can act out the answer in the least amount of time.

Password is a relatively new parlor game. The hostess makes a list of words. Teams of two people compete with each other by trying to guess a word before the other team. One player on each team is given the same word. He must give a one-word clue to his partner. The partner responds with his guess of the word. If it is incorrect, the next team tries the same thing. The one-word clues and answers continue until someone gives the right answers. Example: The word is "paint." Player A says, "brush." His partner, player B, says, "comb." C gives the clue "canvas." His partner, D, guesses "artist." Player A says "oil," and B guesses correctly "paint."

Categories and *anagrams* are pencil and paper games. To play categories, give each participant a sheet of paper with a five-letter word written across the top and five different categories listed down one side. Each person must fill in a word to fit the category under each of the five letters at the top. The word listed must begin with that particular letter. The categories can be any you think of—songs, states, books, authors, brand names, and so on. The first one done or the one with the most words listed within a time limit is the winner.

Anagrams is a game of making a new word from another word by scrambling the letters. It's also possible to see how many words the player can make from one long word. Only the letters used in the original can be repeated and no one letter can be used more times than it is in the original. Example: The word is GARDEN—age, aged, and, anger, are, danger, dare, darn, dear, den, drag, ear, earn, era, erg, gander, gear, grad, grade, grand, nag, ran, rag, rage, rang, range, read, red, and rend.

Activity games

These are games that can be played indoors or out and are physical activity games. Most require equipment that you purchase or make and most require some degree of skill. Games such as darts, table tennis, shuffleboard and badminton can be set up as tournament games with simple elimination. Or they can be played just for fun by whoever feels like playing at the time. There are also many new games being manufactured which lend themselves to party activities.

Treasure hunts or scavenger hunts are team games. Each team, however many you choose, receives a clue which leads to another clue and eventually to a prize, or each team receives a list of items it must find and bring back.

Card games

Card games are usually the entertainment for the entire party or the purpose for the party. Bridge is particularly popular, and evenings or afternoons are often set aside just for playing the game.

Clubs are formed that meet regularly to play. Other card games, played with one or two decks, organized for two to any number, and some having a variety of forms, include hearts, pitch, poker, tripoli, pinochle, and canasta. The varieties of card games are nearly endless so your selection is a wide one.

Commercial games

Several companies manufacture games for individual use, for families, and for large groups. Many, such as Monopoly, have been popular for years and offer hours of fun and provocative competi-

tion. Some, such as Twister, are a little more physically strenuous and are for the limber and uninhibited. Many of the commercial games such as Tip-it, are intended for children, but adults enjoy them every bit as much. The games made specifically for adults are often thought-provoking and require cunning and concentration. Some of these games are attractively packaged to sit in a place of honor on your bookshelf.

For a quiet evening, jigsaw puzzles are ideal. They allow pleasant conversation, are not taxing or strenuous, and come in many, many kinds, sizes, and shapes (round, square, octagonal).

These "bookshelf" games are some of the many manufactured for adults. They are ideal for game parties because they're stimulating and can accommodate different numbers of players.

Party games make clever hostess gifts, too. If you have been a weekend guest and you know your hosts enjoy this form of entertaining, give them an attractive game—they'll use it for years.

RECIPES FOR ENTERTAINING

No party is complete without something to eat or drink. That something might be a four course dinner with a different wine for each course or a coffee and dessert snack. Or it might be simply a tall glass of iced tea on a July afternoon. But there is always something—and it's usually dressed up in its party best.

The recipes selected for *Guide to Entertaining* have been chosen for their party appeal, their adaptability, and their appropriateness to the particular party for which they are suggested. Each one has been listed elsewhere in the book in the menu suggestions given with a certain party and each has been starred to indicate that it appears in the recipe chapter. There are hurry-up selections for those times of last-minute entertaining and there are those that take loving care and patience to complete. And there are many in-between recipes that may become standards in your party notebook.

The recipes given in this chapter are organized by the party with which they are mentioned and in the order in which they appear in the book. Each is also listed in the index under the "Recipe" heading.

This chapter includes, too, a planning guide for a crowd. You'll find common foods, the amounts necessary to purchase to feed from 25 to 50 people, and the approximate size of the servings each will yield.

In the special section, the chapter lists wines and how best to serve them, wine and party punches, common cocktail recipes, and a listing and photograph of useful bar and party equipment. All are designed as a guide to help the hostess understand this phase of entertaining and to have information she may want available at her fingertips.

The editors hope you find convenience-plus in this arrangement of a guide to entertaining and a cook book all in one.

← **When it's your turn** to entertain a crowd, plan to arrange it buffet-style. Guests help themselves to baked ham, scalloped potatoes, and Garden Wheel Salad. The dessert is an Angel Pineapple Torte. The recipes for this lavish buffet appear in the Winter party section on pages 152 and 153.

Cook-At-The-Table

CHINESE HOT POT

¾ pound large raw shrimp, shelled
(about 12 shrimp)
2 uncooked chicken breasts,
skinned and boned, sliced
very thin across grain
½ pound uncooked beef sirloin,
sliced very thin across grain
½ head Chinese cabbage *or* 1 head
lettuce heart, coarsely cubed
1 cup cubed eggplant *or* 1 5-ounce
can water chestnuts, drained and
sliced very thin
1½ cups halved fresh mushrooms
4 cups small spinach leaves, with
stems removed

. . .

6 13¾-ounce cans (10½ cups) *or* 2
46-ounce cans chicken broth
(not condensed)
2 tablespoons monosodium glutamate
1 tablespoon grated gingerroot *or*
1 teaspoon ground ginger

Shortly before cooking time, arrange raw meats and vegetables on large tray or platter and fill bowl with spinach.

In an electric skillet, chafing dish, or Mongolian cooker, heat chicken broth, monosodium glutamate, and ginger to a gentle boil.

Set out bowls of the dunking sauces. Each guest picks up desired food with chopsticks or tongs and drops it into the bubbling broth. When tidbits are cooked, he lifts them out and dips into sauces on plate. (Add more broth if needed.) Makes 6 servings.

CHINESE MUSTARD

Stir ¼ cup boiling water into ¼ cup dry mustard. Add ½ teaspoon salt and 1 tablespoon salad oil. For a more yellow color, add a little turmeric. Makes about ⅓ cup.

GINGER SOY

In a saucepan, combine ½ cup soy sauce and 1½ teaspoons ground ginger. Bring to boiling; serve hot or cold. Makes ½ cup sauce.

PEANUT SAUCE

In a bowl, thoroughly combine ¼ cup chunk-style peanut butter, 2 teaspoons soy sauce, 1½ teaspoons water, ¼ teaspoon sugar, 1 drop bottled hot pepper sauce, and ½ clove garlic, minced. Slowly mix in ¼ cup water till smooth. Makes about ½ cup.

RED SAUCE

Mix 3 tablespoons catsup, 3 tablespoons chili sauce, 1½ tablespoons prepared horseradish, 1 teaspoon lemon juice, and dash bottled hot pepper sauce. Makes ½ cup sauce.

Fall Party

HALIBUT ROYALE

3 tablespoons lemon juice
½ teaspoon paprika
6 halibut steaks
½ cup chopped onion
2 tablespoons butter or margarine
6 green pepper strips

In shallow dish, combine lemon juice, 1 teaspoon salt, and paprika. Add halibut. Marinate for 1 hour (turn after 30 minutes). Cook onion in butter till tender. Place steaks in greased 10x6x1½-inch baking dish. Top with green pepper, and, then sprinkle with onion. Bake at 450° for 10 minutes or till fish flakes easily. Makes 6 servings.

MAPLE SYRUP PIE

3 tablespoons cornstarch
1 cup maple syrup
1 tablespoon butter or margarine
Pastry for 2-crust 8-inch pie
½ cup chopped walnuts

In medium saucepan, gradually stir ½ cup cold water into cornstarch. Add maple syrup. Cook and stir over medium heat till mixture thickens and boils; cook 1 minute more. Add butter. Pour into pastry-lined pie plate. Sprinkle with nuts. Slit and adjust top crust. Seal and flute edges. Bake at 400° for 30 minutes.

Winter Parties

PINEAPPLE REFRESHER

Chill one 46-ounce can pineapple juice. Just before serving, gently stir in three 7-ounce bottles chilled lemon-lime carbonated beverage. Shake in aromatic bitters to taste. Serve over ice. Makes 16 ½-cup servings.

SCALLOPED POTATOES SUPREME

    8 cups thinly sliced pared potatoes
    ¼ cup chopped green pepper
    ¼ cup finely chopped onion
    1 10½-ounce can condensed cream
        of mushroom soup
    1 cup milk
    2 teaspoons salt

In greased 11x7x1½-inch baking dish or 2-quart casserole alternate layers of potatoes, green pepper, and onion. Combine remaining ingredients and dash pepper; pour over.

Cover; bake at 350° for 45 minutes. Uncover and bake 20 to 30 minutes longer or till potatoes are tender. Makes 8 servings.

ANGEL PINEAPPLE TORTE

Have 9 egg whites (1¼ cups) at room temperature. Add 1 tablespoon vanilla, 1 teaspoon cream of tartar, and ½ teaspoon salt. Beat till frothy. Gradually add 3 cups sugar, a small amount at a time, beating till very stiff peaks form and sugar is dissolved (about 10 to 15 minutes).

Cover cookie sheet with plain ungreased brown paper. Using an 8-inch round cake pan as guide, draw 3 circles on the paper. Divide meringue mixture among circles; spread to make 3 smooth flat layers. Bake at 275° for 1½ hours. Turn off heat and let dry in oven (door closed) at least 2 hours or overnight.

Fold one 20½-ounce can crushed pineapple, well drained (1½ cups), and ½ cup chopped maraschino cherries, *well drained*, into 1 cup whipping cream, whipped; spread between layers of meringue. Frost torte with 2 cups whipping cream, whipped. Chill 12 to 24 hours. Serves 12 to 16.

GARDEN WHEEL SALAD

    1 large head cauliflower, cooked
        whole
    3 10-ounce packages frozen asparagus
        spears, cooked
    2 16-ounce cans green beans
    2 bunches (12 to 16) small carrots,
        cooked
    2 10-ounce packages frozen peas,
        cooked
    2 16-ounce cans sliced beets
    2 8-ounce bottles clear French salad
        dressing with herbs and spices
    1 medium onion, thinly sliced and
        separated in rings
      Chutney Dressing

Drain cooked and canned vegetables. Place each in separate dish. Drizzle French dressing over and chill several hours or overnight, turning occasionally.

Line large platter with lettuce. Set cauliflower in center in large lettuce cup; arrange marinated vegetables and onion rings around, spoke fashion. Serve with Chutney Dressing. Makes 16 servings.

CHUTNEY DRESSING

Mix well 1½ cups mayonnaise, ¼ cup chopped chutney, ½ teaspoon curry powder.

SILVER-PLATED SKI-BUM DINNER

    1 large onion, thinly sliced
    1 pound beef chuck, cut in 1-inch
        cubes
    4 medium carrots, thinly sliced
    4 potatoes, pared and cubed
      Snipped parsley
    1 10¾-ounce can beef gravy

Tear off four 16-inch lengths of 18-inch wide heavy foil. Divide onion slices among the 4 lengths; top with meat and vegetables. Sprinkle each with salt, pepper, and parsley, then drizzle with gravy. Pull together opposite corners of foil. Twist top to seal securely, but allow room for expansion of steam. Cook directly on *low* coals about 1 hour or till tender—don't turn. Makes 4 servings.

Spring

ROAST CHICKEN

Rinse a 3- to 4-pound ready-to-cook broiler-fryer. Pat dry with paper towels. Sprinkle cavity with 1 teaspoon salt. For flavor, tuck in some celery leaves and chopped onion if you like. Push ends of drumsticks under strip of skin, if present, or tie to tail. Fold neck skin over back, fasten with skewer. Fold wings across back; tie tips together with cord.

Place breast up on rack in shallow roasting pan (or breast down, if using V-rack). Brush with melted butter or margarine. Roast uncovered at 375° for 1½ to 2¼ hours or till tender, basting occasionally with drippings.

When bird is ⅔ done, snip strip of skin or cord. (If roasted breast down, turn breast up to brown.) Continue roasting till done—thickest part of thigh meat will feel very soft when pressed between fingers (protect fingers with paper towels) and drumstick will move up and down easily. For picnic, cool chicken slightly, then chill promptly. Makes 4 servings.

CURRIED PICNIC SALAD

   6 cups diced cooked potatoes
¼ cup chopped green onions and tops
   2 tablespoons lemon juice
   1 teaspoon celery seed

      • • •

   4 hard-cooked eggs
   1 teaspoon curry powder
   1 cup dairy sour cream
½ cup mayonnaise or salad dressing
   2 teaspoons lemon juice
   1 6-ounce jar marinated artichoke
      hearts*, drained

Combine first 4 ingredients, 1½ teaspoons salt and ½ teaspoon pepper. Separate whites and yolks of hard-cooked eggs; chop whites. Add to potato mixture. Toss lightly and chill.

Mash 2 of the yolks; blend in curry powder, sour cream, mayonnaise, and 2 teaspoons lemon juice. Pour over potatoes. Toss lightly. Sieve remaining yolks over top. Border with marinated artichoke hearts. Keep chilled. Makes 6 to 8 servings.

*Or cook 10-ounce package frozen artichoke hearts. Chill in Italian salad dressing.

CHILLED FRUIT TODDY

Add water to one 6-ounce can frozen tangerine concentrate according to label directions. Stir in one 11-ounce can (1½ cups) pear nectar, chilled, and 1 teaspoon aromatic bitters (or more to taste). To serve, pour fruit toddy over ice cubes in old-fashioned glass. Makes ten ½-cup servings.

LIMED PINEAPPLE-IN-THE-SHELL

   1 fresh pineapple
½ cup sugar
¼ cup lime juice

Leaving the leafy top of pineapple intact, cut a slice off the top to use as a lid.

Run a sharp knife around inside of shell, leaving pineapple shell about ½-inch thick. Cut fruit in wedges. Remove fruit wedge, loosen remaining wedges at bottom with a grapefruit knife. Lift wedges out. Cut fruit in chunks (discard core) and mix with the sugar and lime juice. Spoon the chunks back into the shell and top with the "lid." Hold lid in place with a skewer.

Chill fruit for 3 to 4 hours or overnight. Makes 4 or 5 servings.

Tail-gate Picnic

CARAWAY SKILLET SLAW

   4 slices bacon
¼ cup vinegar
   2 tablespoons sliced green onion
   1 tablespoon brown sugar
   1 teaspoon salt

      • • •

   4 cups shredded cabbage (about ½
      medium head)
   1 teaspoon caraway seed

In skillet, cook bacon till crisp. Remove bacon, drain, and crumble. Measure ¼ cup bacon drippings—return to skillet. Add vinegar, onion, brown sugar, and salt. Pack to carry. Heat through on location. Add cabbage and caraway seed to skillet. Toss mixture lightly. Top with bacon. If desired, garnish with cherry tomatoes. Makes 6 servings.

COUNTRY-STYLE RIBS

4 pounds country-style ribs, cut in serving size pieces
1 tablespoon butter or margarine
1 clove garlic, crushed
½ cup catsup
⅓ cup chili sauce
2 tablespoons brown sugar
2 tablespoons chopped onion
1 tablespoon Worcestershire sauce
1 tablespoon prepared mustard
1 teaspoon celery seed
Dash bottled hot pepper sauce
3 thin lemon slices

Simmer ribs, covered, in salted water to cover till nearly tender, about 1 hour. Meanwhile, prepare barbecue sauce: In saucepan, melt butter or margarine; add garlic and cook 4 to 5 minutes. Add remaining ingredients and ¼ teaspoon salt. Bring to boiling. Drain and chill* or carry to site hot. Grill over medium coals about 11 minutes on each side*, brushing with sauce till well coated. Makes 6 to 8 servings. *If ribs are chilled before grilling, cook 15 to 18 minutes on each side.

CHOCOLATE DAISY CUPCAKES

½ cup butter or margarine
1½ cups sugar
2 eggs
2 cups sifted all-purpose flour
¼ cup cocoa (regular type, dry)
1 teaspoon soda
2 teaspoons instant tea powder
1 cup cold water
1 teaspoon vanilla
1 can chocolate frosting

Cream together butter and sugar till light and fluffy. Add eggs, one at a time, beating well after each. Sift together flour, cocoa, soda, and ½ teaspoon salt. Dissolve tea in the cold water; add vanilla. Alternately add dry ingredients and tea to creamed mixture, beating till smooth after each addition. Line muffin pans with paper or foil cups. Fill each half full. Bake at 350° for 20 minutes. Cool. Frost with chocolate frosting. Arrange whole blanched almonds on each cupcake to make a daisy; add a chocolate candy cake decoration for center. Makes 2 dozen.

Mountain Trout Party

MOUNTAIN RAINBOW TROUT

Further enhance the flavor of the crisp, corn-coated trout with a squeeze of fresh lemon juice—

⅔ cup yellow cornmeal
¼ cup all-purpose flour
2 teaspoons salt
½ teaspoon paprika
• • •
6 large fresh or frozen trout

Combine cornmeal, flour, salt, and paprika. Coat fish. In skillet, heat a little cooking oil over hot coals for about 10 minutes. Cook fish till lightly browned on one side, about 4 minutes; turn and brown on other side about 4 minutes. Cook till fish flakes easily when tested with a fork. (Take care not to overcook.) Makes six servings.

POTATOES WITH CHEF'S CHEESE SAUCE

Carry the refrigerated cheese sauce along to campsite or backyard barbecue in your cooler—

4 tablespoons butter or margarine, softened
4 ounces sharp process American cheese, shredded (1 cup)
½ cup dairy sour cream
1 tablespoon sliced green onion
• • •
5 or 6 medium baking potatoes

Have first four ingredients at room temperature. Whip together butter and cheese with electric beater till light and fluffy. At campsite, stir in sour cream and onion.

Scrub potatoes (for crunchy skins, bake as is; for soft skins, rub with a little cooking oil). Wrap each in square of foil. Bake 45 minutes to 1 hour on grill, or directly on hot coals. When potatoes are done, roll gently under hand to make mealy inside. Cut a crisscross in top of each potato, cutting through foil. Turn back points of foil. Push in ends of potato to fluff; top with cheese mixture. If desired, sprinkle with additional sliced green onion. Makes 5 or 6 servings.

Western Party

India

RANCH HOUSE ROUND STEAK

    3 pounds round steak, cut ½ inch
        thick
    ¼ cup all-purpose flour
    2 teaspoons dry mustard
    ¼ cup salad oil
    1 tablespoon Worcestershire sauce

Cut meat in serving-size pieces; trim excess fat. Slash edges of meat. Combine flour, mustard, 1½ teaspoons salt, and ⅛ teaspoon pepper; coat meat with mixture. (Set aside any remaining flour mixture.) In heavy skillet, brown meat on both sides in hot oil. Add reserved flour mixture to skillet. Combine ½ cup water and Worcestershire; stir into mixture in skillet. Cover tightly. Cook over low heat for 1 to 1¼ hours or till meat is tender. Remove meat to platter.

Skim excess fat from pan juices; drizzle juices over meat. Makes 8 servings.

TEXAS STYLE BEANS

    2 cups pinto beans
    1 cup chopped onion
    ¼ pound salt pork, diced (1 cup)
    1 clove garlic, minced
    2 16-ounce cans (4 cups) tomatoes
    ¾ cup diced green pepper
    6 drops bottled hot pepper sauce
    1 tablespoon sugar
      Perfect Corn Bread

Cover beans with water; soak overnight. Do not drain. Add onion, 2 teaspoons salt, pork, garlic, and dash pepper. Simmer, covered, for 2 hours. Add tomatoes, green pepper, hot pepper sauce, and sugar. Cook, covered, for 3 hours more. Serve over corn bread squares. Serves 9.

Perfect Corn Bread: Sift together 1 cup sifted all-purpose flour, ¼ cup sugar, 4 teaspoons baking powder, and ¾ teaspoon salt. Stir in 1 cup yellow cornmeal. Add 1 cup milk, 2 eggs, and ¼ cup softened shortening. Beat with rotary or electric beater just till smooth, about 1 minute. (Do not overbeat.) Pour into greased 9x9x2-inch baking pan. Bake in hot oven (425°) for 20 to 25 minutes.

CURRIED LAMB

    2 pounds lean lamb, cut in 1-inch
      cubes
    2 tablespoons butter or margarine
    1 cup chopped onion
    1 clove garlic, minced
    1 to 1½ tablespoons curry powder
    1 teaspoon grated fresh gingerroot
      or ½ teaspoon ground ginger
    2 tomatoes, peeled and chopped
    3 tablespoons all-purpose flour

Brown meat in butter; remove from skillet. Add onion and garlic to skillet. Cook till onion is tender but not brown. Return meat to skillet; add curry powder, 1½ teaspoons salt, and gingerroot. Add tomatoes and ¼ cup water. Cover and simmer ¾ to 1 hour, till lamb is tender. Stir occasionally.

Stir in flour; cook and stir till thickened. If desired, serve with cooked rice tossed with raw grated carrot. Serves 6 to 8.

CHAPATTIES

Sift together 2 cups sifted all-purpose flour and 1 teaspoon salt. Add ¼ cup salad oil, mixing well using fork or pastry blender. Stir in 7 tablespoons water, mixing well with hands. (Dough will be very stiff.) Knead 5 to 7 minutes till dough has satiny appearance. Pinch off pieces of dough about 1½ inches in diameter. Roll each into 6-inch circle. Brown on both sides on lightly greased hot griddle. Dot with butter or margarine; serve hot with Curried Lamb. Makes 1 dozen.

Sweden

BEET-HERRING SALAD

1 8-ounce jar (1 cup) pickled
    herring in wine sauce, drained
    and diced
1½ cups diced cooked potatoes
1 16-ounce can diced beets, well
    drained (1½ cups)
½ cup diced unpared apple
¼ cup chopped sweet pickle
¼ cup chopped onion

       • • •

¼ cup vinegar
2 tablespoons sugar
2 tablespoons water
¼ teaspoon salt
    Dash pepper
1 hard-cooked egg

Combine herring, potatoes, beets, apple, pickle, and onion. Blend vinegar, sugar, water, salt, and pepper. Toss with beet mixture. Pack salad into a 4-cup mold or bowl; chill. Drain; unmold on serving plate. Cut egg in wedges; remove yolk. Arrange egg-white wedges spoke fashion atop salad. Sieve yolk over center. Makes 6 to 8 servings.

SHRIMP-CAPERS

For each sandwich, butter 1 thin slice French bread generously. Cover with a ruffled leaf of lettuce. Arrange canned tiny shrimp, overlapping, in two rows atop lettuce. Pipe mayonnaise or salad dressing from pastry tube down center of sandwich. Sprinkle capers over mayonnaise.

EGG-TOMATO-SARDINE SANDWICHES

For each sandwich, butter 1 slice rye bread generously. Mix chopped hard-cooked egg with mayonnaise or salad dressing to moisten; spread on buttered bread. Arrange canned sardines and small tomato wedges atop egg. Garnish with parsley or dill sprigs.

HAM PINWHEEL SANDWICHES

Spread 8 slices whole-wheat bread with mayonnaise; top with shredded lettuce (1⅓ cups). Blend one 3-ounce package cream cheese, softened, and 1 teaspoon horseradish, adding milk if necessary to make mixture of spreading consistency. Spread evenly on 4 slices Danish-style boiled ham. Roll up tightly. Slice each ham roll into tiny pinwheels. Arrange pinwheels on shredded lettuce in diagonal line, 5 per sandwich. Serves 8.

RUM PUDDING

Delicate custard-like dessert with tart raspberry topper—

¼ teaspoon salt
3 egg yolks
6 tablespoons sugar
1 envelope (1 tablespoon)
    unflavored gelatin
⅔ cup cold milk
3 tablespoons rum
1 cup whipping cream, whipped
    Raspberry Sauce

Add salt to egg yolks; beat till thick and lemon-colored. Gradually beat in sugar. Soften gelatin in milk; heat till gelatin dissolves; cool slightly. Add milk mixture gradually to egg yolk mixture, beating constantly. Add rum. Chill till partially set. Fold in whipped cream; turn into individual molds. Chill till set, about 4 hours. Unmold and top with Raspberry Sauce. Serves 6.

Raspberry Sauce: Blend ¼ cup sugar and 1 tablespoon cornstarch; stir in one 10-ounce package frozen raspberries, thawed, and ⅓ cup water. Cook, stirring constantly, till mixture thickens and boils. Cook 2 minutes more. Push through sieve; chill. Makes 1 cup sauce.

Polynesia Party

KONA CHICKEN

- 1 tablespoon curry powder
- 1 cup finely chopped pared apples
- 1 tablespoon butter or margarine
- 1 medium onion, minced (½ cup)
- 1 cup sliced celery
- ½ cup sliced fresh *or* one 3-ounce can sliced mushrooms, drained
- ½ cup condensed beef broth
- 2 tablespoons cornstarch
- 1 cup light cream
- 1 cup milk
- 2 cups diced cooked chicken
- 1 teaspoon monosodium glutamate
  Seasoned mashed potatoes

Cook curry powder and apple in butter till apple is soft; stir in next three ingredients. Add beef broth; bring to boiling. Combine cornstarch and 2 tablespoons water; add with cream and milk to first mixture. Cook and stir till mixture thickens. Stir in chicken, seasonings, and teaspoon salt. Spoon into coconut shells or 2-quart casserole. Decorate coconut husk with hot mashed potatoes squeezed through a pastry tube. Bake at 450° for 10 to 12 minutes. Serves 5 or 6.

BROILED CHICKEN

Split two 2- to 2½-pound ready-to cook broiler-fryer chickens in half lengthwise or in quarters. Brush with melted butter or salad oil. Season with 2 teaspoons salt, dash pepper, and ½ teaspoon monosodium glutamate. Place skin side down in a single layer in broiler pan without rack. Broil 5 to 7 inches from heat about 25 minutes, or till lightly browned. Brush occasionally with melted butter. Turn skin side up and broil 15 to 20 minutes, or till drumstick moves easily and thickest part of chicken feels very soft. Makes 4 servings.

BAKED BANANAS

Leaving skins on, bake 4 firm, green-tipped bananas at 300° about 30 minutes, or until fork tender. Serve with skins on. Let guests peel and salt to taste. Makes 4 servings.

WAIKIKI SALAD

Heap lush tropical fruits high in a pineapple shell. Keep it cool on a bed of crushed ice and tuck in a flower.

BEACH BOY PUNCH

Mix 1 quart cranberry juice, juice of two lemons, and 1 pint orange juice; pour into punch bowl over cake of ice. Add 2 quarts chilled ginger ale. Makes about 4 quarts.

BATTER-FRIED SHRIMP

Combine 1 cup sifted all-purpose flour, ½ teaspoon sugar, ½ teaspoon salt, 1 slightly beaten egg, 1 cup ice water, and 2 tablespoons salad oil. Beat smooth. Shell 2 pounds fresh or frozen shrimp, leaving last section and tail intact. Butterfly shrimp by cutting almost through at center back without severing tail end; remove black vein.

Dry shrimp well. Dip into batter; fry in deep hot fat (375°) till golden. Drain. Serve with sauces (see page 152).

WATER CHESTNUTS WITH CHICKEN LIVERS

Wash fresh water chestnuts thoroughly and slice each in thirds. Or use canned ones.

Cut chicken livers in slices slightly larger than chestnut slices; dip in soy sauce.

Using two slices of chicken liver and one of chestnut, make a sandwich. Wrap in thin slice of bacon, skewer with wooden pick, and fry in deep hot fat (375°) 2 or 3 minutes.

CHINESE PEAS WITH WATER CHESTNUTS

Heat 1 tablespoon salad oil in skillet; fry ⅓ cup finely chopped raw pork. Add 2 cups Chinese green peas, ½ cup finely sliced water chestnuts, and 1 teaspoon monosodium glutamate. Add 1 cup chicken broth.

Steam, covered, over high heat about 3 minutes. Combine 1 tablespoon cornstarch with 2 tablespoons cold water. Push vegetables to one side; add cornstarch mixture to broth. Cook and stir till slightly thick. Salt to taste. Makes 3 to 4 servings.

Oriental Party

SUKIYAKI

If the party is outside, cook in a real wok pan. These basin-shaped saucepans are found in some Oriental shops. To cook, place the wok on its base over a hibachi or other grill. Indoors use as a skillet.

2 tablespoons salad oil

• • •

1 pound beef tenderloin, sliced
    paper-thin across the grain

• • •

2 tablespoons sugar
1 teaspoon monosodium glutamate

• • •

½ cup beef stock *or* canned
    condensed beef broth
⅓ cup soy sauce
2 cups 2-inch length bias-cut
    green onions
1 cup 1-inch bias-cut celery slices

• • •

1 cup thinly sliced fresh mushrooms
1 5-ounce can water chestnuts,
    drained and thinly sliced
1 5-ounce can bamboo shoots,
    drained
5 cups small spinach leaves
1 1-pound can bean sprouts, drained
12 to 16 ounces bean curd, cubed*
    (optional)
2 to 4 ounces dry bean threads
    (optional)

Prepare bean threads ahead by soaking 2 hours in cold water; drain.

Just before cooking time, arrange meat and vegetables attractively on large platter. Have small containers of sugar, monosodium glutamate, soy sauce, and beef stock handy. For "toss-stirring" you'll want to use two tools at once—big spoon and fork.

Preheat large skillet or Oriental saucepan; add oil. Add beef and cook quickly, turning it over and over, 1 to 2 minutes or just till browned. Sprinkle meat with sugar and monosodium glutamate. Combine beef stock and soy sauce; pour over. Push meat to one side. Let the soy sauce mixture bubble.

Keeping in separate groups, add onion and celery. Continue cooking and toss-stirring each group over high heat about 1 minute; push to one side. Again keeping in separate groups, add mushrooms, chestnuts, bamboo shoots, spinach, bean sprouts, and bean curd. Cook and stir each food just till heated through. Let guests help themselves to some of everything. Serve with rice. Pass soy sauce. Makes 4 servings.

*Bean curd (tofu) may be found at Japanese food shops, or obtained from mail-order houses that specialize in Oriental foods.

CHAWAN-MUSHI

A hot custard soup perfect for a party opener—

8 raw shrimp, peeled and deveined
8 spinach leaves, cut in 1½-inch pieces
½ cup sliced mushrooms
8 water chestnuts, sliced

• • •

2 slightly beaten eggs
2 cups chicken broth
½ teaspoon salt

Make small slit in each shrimp; pull tail through. Wilt spinach in hot water, drain. Line up 8 Chawan-Mushi cups or 5-ounce custard cups. In each, place shrimp, spinach, mushrooms, and water chestnuts. Combine eggs, chicken broth, and salt; pour into cups; cover with lids or foil. Set cups on rack in Dutch oven; pour hot water around cups 1-inch deep; cover to steam. Over medium heat, bring water *slowly* to simmering; reduce heat and cook about 7 minutes more or till knife inserted off center comes out clean. Top each custard with ¼ teaspoon soy sauce and a thin twist of lemon peel.

Grecian Feast

MOUSSAKA

2 medium eggplants

. . .

1 pound ground beef
1 cup chopped onion
¼ cup Burgundy
¼ cup water
2 tablespoons snipped parsley
1 tablespoon tomato paste
1 teaspoon salt
Dash pepper
1 slice bread, torn into crumbs
2 beaten eggs
1 ounce sharp process American
cheese, shredded (¼ cup)
Dash ground cinnamon

. . .

3 tablespoons butter or margarine
3 tablespoons all-purpose flour
1½ cups milk
½ teaspoon salt
Dash pepper
Dash ground nutmeg
1 beaten egg

. . .

1 ounce sharp process American
cheese shredded (¼ cup)

Pare eggplants; cut into slices ½ inch thick.
Sprinkle with a little salt and set aside. In
skillet, brown meat with onion; drain off any
excess fat. Add wine, water, parsley, tomato
paste, 1 teaspoon salt, and dash pepper. Simmer till liquid is nearly absorbed. Cool; stir
in half the bread crumbs, 2 beaten eggs, ¼
cup cheese, and ground cinnamon.

In saucepan, melt butter or margarine; stir
in flour. Add milk; cook and stir till thickened
and bubbly. Add ½ teaspoon salt, dash pepper, and ground nutmeg. Add a little of the
hot sauce to 1 beaten egg; return to hot mixture. Cook over low heat 2 minutes, stirring
constantly. Brown eggplant slices on both
sides in a little hot oil.

Sprinkle bottom of 12x7½x2-inch baking
dish with remaining bread crumbs. Cover
with a layer of eggplant slices; spoon on all of
meat mixture. Arrange remaining eggplant
over meat mixture. Pour milk-egg sauce over
all. Top with remaining cheese. Bake at
350° about 45 minutes. Makes 6 to 8 servings.

SALATA

1 head lettuce, shredded (about 6
cups)
3 tomatoes, peeled and chopped
1 large unpared cucumber, chopped
1 bunch watercress, snipped
(1½ cups)
1 medium green pepper, chopped
4 green onions, finely chopped
(⅛ cup)
¼ cup sliced Greek olives *or*
ripe olives
3 tablespoons lemon juice
1 teaspoon salt

. . .

⅓ cup olive oil

Combine lettuce, tomatoes, cucumber, watercress, green pepper, and green onion. Add
olives, lemon juice, and salt; toss together.
Mound on platter; garnish with tomato
wedges, cucumber slices, and Greek olives, if
desired. Pour olive oil over all. Allow to stand
15 minutes to blend flavors. Serves 8 to 10.

KARIDOPITA

4 egg yolks
½ cup sugar
1 teaspoon shredded orange peel
½ teaspoon shredded lemon peel
2 tablespoons orange juice
1½ tablespoons cognac
1½ cups ground walnuts
¼ cup fine dry bread crumbs
1 teaspoon baking powder
¼ teaspoon ground cinnamon
⅛ teaspoon ground cloves
4 egg whites
¼ teaspoon cream of tartar

Beat egg yolks till light; gradually add sugar,
beating till thick. Stir in orange and lemon
peels, orange juice, and cognac. Combine
ground walnuts, bread crumbs, baking powder, cinnamon, and cloves. Stir in egg yolk
mixture. Beat egg whites with cream of tartar
till stiff peaks form. Fold gently into nut mixture till well distributed. Bake in a well-
greased 8x8x2-inch baking pan in moderate
oven (350°) for about 30 minutes. Cut in small
squares. If desired, serve with whipped cream
and shredded orange peel.

KOURABIEDES

Butter Cookies—

1 cup butter or margarine
⅓ cup sifted confectioners'
  sugar
1 tablespoon cognac
1 teaspoon vanilla
2 cups sifted all-purpose flour
  Whole cloves

Cream butter thoroughly. Add sugar gradually, creaming well. Add cognac and vanilla. Gradually work in flour to make a soft dough. Chill 2½ to 3 hours. Pinch off small pieces of dough and shape into oblong cookies. Center each with a whole clove. Bake on ungreased cookie sheet at 325° for 25 to 30 minutes. (Cookies will not be brown.) Cool on cookie sheet. Sift additional confectioners' sugar over cookies, being careful to coat each cookie evenly and generously. Makes about 2 dozen.

TYROPITAKIA

Cheese Pastries—

1½ cups sifted all-purpose flour
1 cup shredded provolone cheese
½ cup butter or margarine
3 tablespoons milk
1 slightly beaten egg

Combine flour and cheese; cut in butter. Stir in milk and mix well. Divide dough into 24 pieces. Roll each piece into a 5-inch strip. Shape strips into wreaths on ungreased cookie sheet. Brush tops of pastries with the slightly beaten egg. Bake at 350° for 20 to 25 minutes or till lightly browned. Makes 2 dozen.

TAMALE PIE

1 pound ground beef
1 cup chopped onion
1 cup chopped green pepper
• • •
2 8-ounce cans tomato sauce
1 12-ounce can (1½ cups) whole
  kernel corn, drained
½ cup pitted ripe olives, chopped
1 clove garlic, minced
1 tablespoon sugar
1 teaspoon salt
2 to 3 teaspoons chili powder
  Dash pepper
6 ounces sharp process American
  cheese, shredded (1½ cups)
• • •
¾ cup yellow cornmeal
1 tablespoon butter or margarine

Cook meat, onion, and green pepper in a large skillet till meat is lightly browned and vegetables are tender. Stir in tomato sauce, corn, olives, garlic, sugar, salt, chili powder, and pepper. Simmer 20 to 25 minutes, or until thick. Add cheese; stir till melted. Turn into greased 9x9x2-inch baking dish.

To make cornmeal topper, stir cornmeal and ½ teaspoon salt into 2 cups cold water. Cook and stir till thick. Add butter; mix well. Spoon over *hot* meat mixture. Bake casserole at 375° about 40 minutes. Makes 6 servings.

HOT MEXICAN BEAN DIP

1 28-ounce can (3¼ cups)
  pork and beans in tomato sauce,
  sieved
2 ounces sharp process American
  cheese, shredded (½ cup)
1 teaspoon garlic salt
1 teaspoon chili powder
½ teaspoon salt
  Dash cayenne pepper
2 teaspoons vinegar
2 teaspoons Worcestershire sauce
½ teaspoon liquid smoke
4 slices bacon, crisp-cooked,
  drained, and crumbled

Combine all ingredients except bacon; heat through. Top with bacon. Serve with corn chips or potato chips. Makes 3 cups.

Mid-Morning Brunch

DEVILED SCRAMBLED EGGS

12 eggs
¾ cup milk or light cream
1½ teaspoons salt
1½ teaspoons dry mustard
¾ teaspoon Worcestershire sauce
¼ cup butter or margarine
1 3-ounce can whole mushrooms, drained

With a fork, beat together eggs, milk, seasonings, and dash pepper. Heat butter in skillet; pour in egg mixture; turn heat to low. When mixture starts to set, lift and turn cooked portions with wide spatula. Continue cooking till eggs are cooked throughout but still glossy and moist. Serve with mushrooms. Serves 8.

HERBED TOMATO SLICES

Dot tomato halves with butter, season, and sprinkle with crushed herbs. Broil, cut side up, 3 inches from heat about 5 minutes or till heated through (don't turn).

Luncheon

LOBSTER-SHRIMP CHOWDER

¼ cup chopped celery
2 tablespoons finely chopped onion
2 tablespoons butter or margarine
1 10½-ounce can condensed cream of potato soup
1 10½-ounce can condensed cream of mushroom soup
1 soup can milk
1 cup light cream
1 5-ounce can lobster, drained
1 4½-ounce can shrimp, drained
¼ cup dry sherry
1 tablespoon snipped parsley

Cook celery and onion in butter or margarine till tender but not brown. Stir in the potato soup, mushroom soup, milk, cream, lobster, shrimp, dry sherry, and snipped parsley. Heat through. Makes 4 to 6 servings.

PINEAPPLE DELIGHT CAKE

This party-pretty dessert can be made ahead to save you hostessing time—

1 package 2-layer-size yellow cake mix
1 3¾- or 3⅝-ounce package *instant* vanilla pudding mix
1 13½-ounce can (1⅜ cups) crushed pineapple, undrained
1 2-ounce package dessert topping mix

Prepare and bake two 8- or 9-inch layers from cake mix according to package directions; cool. Stir pudding mix into crushed pineapple. Prepare dessert topping according to package directions; fold in pineapple mixture. Spread about 1½ cups frosting on bottom cake layer; top with second layer. Frost sides of cake lightly; top cake with remaining frosting. Garnish with halved pineapple slices and maraschino cherries. Chill till serving time.

Tea

TUNA ROUNDS

Combine one 6½- or 7-ounce can tuna, drained; ½ cup mayonnaise or salad dressing; one 5-ounce can water chestnuts, drained and chopped; 1 tablespoon minced onion; 1 teaspoon lemon juice; 1 teaspoon soy sauce; and ½ teaspoon curry powder. Mix thoroughly. Spread mixture on slices of small rounds of rye bread. Trim each with a pimiento-stuffed green olive slice. Makes about 36 open-faced tea sandwiches.

NUT BREAD SANDWICHES

Blend softened cream cheese with orange marmalade, cranberry jelly, or crushed pineapple. Spread on nut bread.

SUGAR COOKIES

⅔ cup shortening
¾ cup granulated sugar
1 teaspoon vanilla

• • •

1 egg
4 teaspoons milk
2 cups sifted all-purpose flour
1½ teaspoons baking powder
¼ teaspoon salt

Thoroughly cream shortening, sugar, and vanilla. Add egg; beat till light and fluffy. Stir in milk. Sift together dry ingredients; blend into creamed mixture. Divide dough in half. Chill 1 hour.

On lightly floured surface, roll to ⅛ inch thickness.* Cut in desired shapes with cutters. Bake on greased cookie sheet at 375° about 6 to 8 minutes. Cool slightly; remove from pan. Makes 2 dozen.

*Chill other half till ready to use.

THUMBPRINTS

⅔ cup butter or margarine
⅛ cup granulated sugar
2 egg yolks
1 teaspoon vanilla
1½ cups sifted all-purpose flour
2 slightly beaten egg whites
¾ cup finely chopped walnuts
36 candied cherry halves

Cream together butter or margarine and sugar till fluffy. Add egg yolks, vanilla, and ½ teaspoon salt; beat well. Gradually add flour, mixing well. Shape dough in ¾-inch balls; dip in egg whites, then roll in walnuts. Place 1 inch apart on greased cookie sheet. Press down center of each with thumb. Bake in moderate oven (350°) for 15 to 17 minutes or till done. Cool slightly; remove from sheet and cool on rack. Top centers with candied cherry halves just before serving. Makes about 3 dozen thumbprint cookies.

LEMON TEA CAKES

1½ teaspoons vinegar
½ cup milk
½ cup butter or margarine
¾ cup granulated sugar
1 egg
1 teaspoon shredded lemon peel
1¾ cups sifted all-purpose flour
1 teaspoon baking powder
¼ teaspoon soda
Lemon Glaze

Stir vinegar into milk. Cream butter and sugar till fluffy. Beat in egg and peel. Sift together dry ingredients and ½ teaspoon salt; add to creamed mixture alternately with milk, beating after each addition. Drop from teaspoon 2 inches apart on ungreased cookie sheet. Bake at 350° for 12 to 14 minutes. Remove at once from sheet. Brush tops with glaze.

Lemon Glaze: Mix ¾ cup granulated sugar and ¼ cup lemon juice. Makes 4 dozen.

LIME FROSTED PUNCH

1 29-ounce can pineapple-grapefruit drink, chilled
⅔ cup lemon juice
3 ½-ounce envelopes unsweetened lemon-lime soft drink powder
2 cups sugar
2 pints lime sherbet
4 7-ounce bottles lemon-lime carbonated beverage, chilled

In punch bowl, combine first four ingredients with 2 quarts cold water. Stir till all is dissolved. Top with spoonfuls of sherbet. Pour in carbonated beverage. Serves 30 to 35.

Open House

COCONUT MACAROONS

    2 egg whites
      Dash salt
    ½ teaspoon vanilla
    ⅔ cup sugar
    1 3½-ounce can (1⅓ cups)
      flaked coconut

Beat egg whites with salt and vanilla till soft peaks form. Gradually add sugar, beating till stiff peaks form. Fold in coconut. Drop by rounded teaspoons onto greased cookie sheet. Bake in slow oven (325°) for about 20 minutes. Makes about 1½ dozen cookies.

CAFE ARUBA

A tempting brew rich with the fragrance and flavor of fresh oranges—

    3 cups hot double-strength coffee
    ¼ cup orange peel cut in very
      thin strips
    1 orange, peeled and sliced
    1 tablespoon sugar
    1 teaspoon aromatic bitters
    ½ cup whipping cream, whipped
      and sweetened to taste

Measure hot coffee into glass pot. Add orange peel and slices. Let mixture steep over low heat for about 15 minutes. Add sugar and bitters. Do not boil. Strain and pour into warmed, footed glasses. Top with sweetened whipped cream. Makes 4 or 5 servings.

CAPPUCCINO

    ¼ cup instant espresso or instant
      dark-roast coffee
    2 cups boiling water
    ½ cup whipping cream, whipped
      Ground cinnamon *or* nutmeg

Dissolve coffee in boiling water; pour into cups. Pass sugar, if desired. Top each with a big spoonful of whipped cream; dash with ground cinnamon *or* nutmeg. Fold cream into coffee till frothy. Makes 6 or 7 small servings.

TRI-LEVEL BROWNIES

This variation of the ever-popular brownie is a perfect go-with for Cappuccino and Cafe Aruba or Irish Coffee—

    ½ cup sifted all-purpose flour
    ¼ teaspoon soda
    ¼ teaspoon salt
    1 cup quick-cooking rolled oats
    ½ cup brown sugar
    ½ cup butter or margarine, melted
          •   •   •
    1 square (1 ounce) unsweetened
      chocolate, melted *or* 1 envelope
      no-melt unsweetened chocolate
    ¼ cup butter or margarine, melted
    ¾ cup granulated sugar
    1 egg
    ⅔ cup sifted all-purpose flour
    ¼ teaspoon baking powder
    ¼ teaspoon salt
    ¼ cup milk
    ½ teaspoon vanilla
    ½ cup chopped walnuts
          •   •   •
    1 square (1 ounce) unsweetened
      chocolate
    2 tablespoons butter or margarine
    1½ cups sifted confectioners' sugar
    1 teaspoon vanilla

For bottom layer: Sift together ½ cup flour, soda, and ¼ teaspoon salt; combine with rolled oats and brown sugar. Stir in ½ cup melted butter or margarine. Pat mixture in bottom of 11x7x1½-inch baking pan and bake in moderate oven (350°) 10 minutes.

For middle layer: Combine chocolate, ¼ cup melted butter, and granulated sugar; add egg and beat well. Sift together ⅔ cup flour, baking powder, and ¼ teaspoon salt; add alternately with milk and vanilla to chocolate mixture. Fold in nuts. Spread batter over baked layer. Return to oven and bake in moderate oven (350°) for about 25 minutes.

For Frosting: Combine the square of unsweetened chocolate and the butter or margarine in a small saucepan. Stir over low heat till chocolate melts. Remove from heat and add confectioners' sugar and vanilla. Blend in enough hot water (about 2 tablespoons) to make almost pourable consistency. Spread over cooled brownies. Top with walnut halves. Makes 16 large bars.

PECAN TASSIES

  1 3-ounce package cream cheese
  ½ cup butter or margarine
  1 cup sifted all-purpose flour

      • • •

  1 egg
  ¾ cup brown sugar
  1 tablespoon butter or
     margarine, softened
  1 teaspoon vanilla
     Dash salt
  ⅔ cup coarsely broken pecans

Cheese pastry: Let cream cheese and ½ cup butter or margarine soften at room temperature; blend together. Stir in flour; chill about 1 hour. Shape in 2 dozen 1-inch balls; place in ungreased 1¾-inch muffin pans. Press dough against bottoms and sides.

Pecan filling: Beat together egg, brown sugar, 1 tablespoon butter, vanilla, and dash salt just till smooth. Divide half the pecans among pastry-lined pans; add egg mixture and top with remaining pecans. Bake in slow oven (325°) for 25 minutes or till filling is set. Cool before removing from pans. Makes 2 dozen.

Teen Supper

TAMALE HERO SANDWICHES

Hearty chili and cheese sandwiches will be teen favorites served with corn chips—

  3 hero buns or 4 or 5-inch chunks of
     French bread
  ¼ cup chopped green pepper
  1 tablespoon instant minced onion
  1 15-ounce can chili with beans

      • • •

  1 15-ounce can tamales
  3 ounces sharp natural Cheddar
     cheese, shredded (¾ cup)

Slice hero buns in half lengthwise and toast. Add green pepper and onion to chili; spread buns with chili mixture. Split tamales lengthwise and arrange atop chili. Sprinkle with shredded cheese. Place under broiler for about 10 minutes or till cheese melts and sandwiches are heated through. Makes 6 open-face sandwiches.

Fondue Supper

BEEF FONDUE

     Salad oil for cooking
  1½ pounds trimmed beef tenderloin,
      cut in ¾-inch cubes
     Buttered Mushrooms
     Bottled Dijon-style Mustard
     Sour Cream Blue Cheese Sauce
     Bordelaise Sauce
     Red Sauce (see page 152)

Pour salad oil in saucepan or beef fondue cooker to no more than ½ capacity or to depth of 2 inches. Heat to 425° or till oil begins to bubble. Carefully transfer to cooker; place over alcohol burner or canned heat. Have beef cubes at room temperature in serving bowls. Set out small bowls of butters and sauces. Each guest spears a beef cube with fondue fork, then holds it in the hot oil until cooked to desired doneness. Transfer meat to a dinner fork; dip in sauce on plate. Serves 4.

BUTTERED MUSHROOMS

Melt 2 tablespoons butter or margarine in skillet. Add one 6-ounce can sliced mushrooms, drained (about 1 cup) *or* 1 pint fresh mushrooms, sliced. Cook over moderate heat, stirring occasionally, until evenly browned. Season with salt and pepper.

SOUR CREAM BLUE CHEESE

Combine 1 cup dairy sour cream, ¼ cup crumbled blue cheese, and a dash of Worcestershire sauce. Chill. Make about 1⅛ cups.

BORDELAISE SAUCE

In saucepan, cook ½ cup fresh mushrooms, chopped, in 1 tablespoon butter till tender, about 4 minutes. Mix 3 tablespoons cornstarch with 2 cups cool beef stock. Stir into mushrooms. Cook and stir till boiling. Add 3 tablespoons red wine, 2 tablespoons lemon juice, 2 teaspoons dried tarragon, crushed, and a dash pepper; simmer 5 to 10 minutes. Makes 2¼ cups sauce.

Semi-formal Dinner

PINEAPPLE SHRUB

2 cups pineapple juice
1 cup apple juice
2 tablespoons lemon juice
1 pint pineapple sherbet
Fresh mint

Combine pineapple, apple, and lemon juices; pour into juice glasses and chill. Just before serving, top each glass with a small scoop of pineapple sherbet and a sprig of fresh mint. Makes 6 to 8 servings.

BRACE OF DUCKLINGS WITH CRANBERRY SAUCE

2 3½- to 4-pound ready-to-cook ducklings
1 10½-ounce can condensed beef broth (about 1¼ cups)
¾ cup cranberry juice cocktail
2 tablespoons butter or margarine
2 tablespoons sugar
2 tablespoons vinegar
1 tablespoon cornstarch
1 tablespoon cranberry juice cocktail

Place ducklings, breast side up, on rack in shallow roasting pan. Prick skin well. Roast, uncovered, in moderate oven (375°) for 1½ hours. Increase oven temperature to 425° and roast 15 minutes more or till tender. Meanwhile, place neck and giblets in saucepan. Add beef broth and simmer, covered, for 1 hour. Strain broth; serve giblets with duck.

To strained broth, add ¾ cup cranberry juice cocktail; cook till reduced to 1 cup. In small pan, melt butter or margarine. Blend in sugar; cook and stir till brown. Add vinegar and cranberry-broth mixture. Remove ducklings from roasting pan to warm serving platter. Skim fat from meat juices. Add juices to cranberry-broth mixture.

Blend cornstarch with 1 tablespoon cranberry juice cocktail; stir into sauce. Cook and stir till sauce is thick and bubbly; simmer 1 to 2 minutes. Pass with duckling. Garnish with parsley and kumquat flowers. Makes approximately 8 servings.

CURRY SALAD DRESSING

1½ teaspoons liquid beef-flavored gravy base*
1 cup mayonnaise or salad dressing
½ teaspoon curry powder
Bibb lettuce
1 large avocado, peeled and sliced

Thoroughly combine beef gravy base, 3 tablespoons hot water, mayonnaise, and curry powder. Chill. Serve on Bibb lettuce; garnish with avocado slices. (Dip slices in lemon juice to keep color bright.) Serves 8.

*Or use 1 beef bouillon cube dissolved in 3 tablespoons *boiling* water.

WILD RICE AND MUSHROOMS

1 3-ounce can (⅔ cup) broiled sliced mushrooms
1 13¾-ounce can chicken broth (about 1¾ cups)
2 medium onions, finely chopped
½ cup uncooked wild rice
1 cup uncooked long-grain rice
2 tablespoons butter or margarine
2 tablespoons snipped parsley

Drain mushrooms, reserving liquid. In a saucepan, combine mushroom liquid and broth; add onion and bring to boiling. Add washed wild rice; reduce heat and simmer, covered, for 20 minutes. Add long-grain rice; return to boiling. Reduce heat and simmer, covered, for 20 minutes longer or till rice is tender. Toss in mushrooms and butter; heat through. Add parsley. Makes 8 servings.

MINCEMEAT-ICE CREAM TARTS

1 quart vanilla ice cream
1 cup prepared mincemeat
1 teaspoon grated orange peel
8 baked tart shells
½ cup whipping cream, whipped
Toasted slivered almonds to garnish

Stir ice cream just to soften; fold in mincemeat and orange peel. Fill tart shells; freeze. Just before serving, top each with whipped cream; garnish with almonds. Makes approximately 8 servings.

Cocktail Party

SPICY BEEF DIP

1 pound ground beef
½ cup chopped onion
1 clove garlic, minced
1 8-ounce can (1 cup) tomato sauce
¼ cup catsup
¾ teaspoon dried oregano leaves, crushed
1 teaspoon sugar
1 8-ounce package cream cheese, softened
⅓ cup grated parmesan cheese

Cook ground beef, onion, and garlic till beef is lightly browned and onion is tender. Stir in tomato sauce, catsup, oregano, and sugar. Cover; simmer gently for 10 minutes. Spoon off excess fat. Remove from heat and add cream cheese and parmesan; stir till cream cheese has melted and is well-combined. Serve warm. Makes 3 cups dip.

SHRIMP IN JACKETS

1 pound frozen medium, shelled shrimp, thawed
½ teaspoon garlic salt
¾ pound bacon (about 15 slices)

Sprinkle shrimp with garlic salt; wrap each in ⅓ slice bacon. Arrange on broiler rack. Broil 3 to 4 inches from heat just till bacon is crisp and browned, 8 to 10 minutes, turning occasionally. Makes about 40.

CRANBERRY GLOGG

Tie 6 whole cloves; 6 inches stick cinnamon; and 4 whole cardamom, shelled, in a cheesecloth bag. Place in saucepan. Add 2 cups cranberry juice cocktail, 1 cup light raisins, and ¼ cup sugar; bring to boiling. Simmer, uncovered, for 10 minutes. Remove spices; cool punch.

Before serving, add 2 cups cranberry juice and 2 cups port wine; heat to almost boiling. Pour into a heat-proof pitcher and serve in mugs or punch cups, adding a few of the raisins to each serving. Makes about 6 cups.

EDAM SAGE SPREAD

1 whole Edam cheese, about 8 ounces
1 cup dairy sour cream
1 teaspoon ground sage
Dash onion powder

Using a sawtooth cut, remove top of whole Edam cheese. Carefully scoop out cheese, leaving a thin shell. Finely chop cheese; mix with sour cream, sage, and onion powder. Spoon into cheese shell; chill thoroughly.

ANTIPASTO TRAY

Fresh Relish Italiano: Thinly slice tomatoes, cucumbers, and onions; separate onion in rings. Pour Italian salad dressing over. Sprinkle with salt and freshly ground pepper. Chill a few hours. Spoon dressing over again.

Avocado Cuts with Salami: Dip slices of ripe avocado in bottled French salad dressing or Italian salad dressing. Alternate avocado with thin slices of salami.

Olive-stuffed Eggs: Peel 5 hard-cooked eggs; halve lengthwise. Remove yolks, mash, and combine with 2 tablespoons *each* mayonnaise and chopped ripe olives, 2 teaspoons vinegar, and 1 teaspoon prepared mustard. Season to taste. Fill whites; chill. Garnish.

Marinated Artichoke Hearts: Cook one 8- or 9-ounce package frozen artichoke hearts following package directions; drain. (Or drain canned artichoke hearts; halve.) Mix 2 tablespoons *each* lemon juice and olive oil; 1 clove garlic, crushed; ¼ teaspoon salt; and dash pepper. Pour over artichokes. Chill; spoon marinade over a few times. At serving time, drain; dash with paprika. Tuck in thin lemon slices between the artichoke halves.

Tonno al Limone: Chill one 7-ounce can solid-pack tuna. Open can and carefully slide the wheel of tuna out onto serving dish. Squeeze juice of ½ lemon over top. Trim with lemon slice and watercress.

Late-Night Supper

SHRIMP QUICHE

    4 ounces process Swiss cheese, shredded (1 cup)
    4 ounces Gruyere cheese, shredded, (1 cup)
    1 tablespoon all-purpose flour
    3 eggs
    1 cup light cream
    ½ teaspoon prepared mustard
    ¼ teaspoon Worcestershire sauce
    Dash bottled hot pepper sauce
    Unbaked pastry for 6 tart shells
    1 10-ounce package frozen peeled, and deveined shrimp, thawed and diced (about 1 cup)

Toss together cheeses and flour. Beat together next 5 ingredients, ¼ teaspoon salt, and dash pepper. Line individual bakers with pastry. Divide ¾ of the cheese mixture among pastry-lined bakers; add shrimp and remaining cheese. Pour in egg mixture. Bake at 400° about 30 minutes or till knife inserted off center comes out clean. Serves 6.

RHUBARB CUP

    Drain one 11-ounce can mandarin oranges, reserving syrup. In saucepan, combine reserved syrup, ½ cup sugar, and ¾ pound rhubarb, cut in 1-inch pieces (3 cups). Bring to boiling; cover and cook over low heat till rhubarb is tender, about 5 minutes. Remove from heat. Stir in mandarin oranges. Chill. Spoon into sherbets; top each with a dollop of whipped cream. Makes 6 servings.

HEARTS OF PALM SALAD

    ⅓ cup salad oil
    2 tablespoons lemon juice
    2 tablespoons finely chopped pimiento-stuffed green olives
    1 tablespoon finely chopped onion
    1 tablespoon finely chopped celery
    1 teaspoon sugar
    ½ teaspoon aromatic bitters
    ¼ teaspoon paprika
    1 14-ounce can hearts of palm, drained and sliced
    6 cups torn Bibb lettuce

Combine first 8 ingredients and ½ teaspoon salt; beat well. Chill. At serving time, toss together hearts of palm and lettuce in salad bowl. Add dressing; toss. Makes 6 servings.

SUGAR-PECAN CRISPS

    ¾ cup butter or margarine
    ⅔ cup sugar
    1 egg
    1 teaspoon vanilla
    ¼ teaspoon salt
    1¾ cups sifted all-purpose flour
    ½ cup finely chopped pecans

Cream together butter or margarine and sugar till light. Beat in egg, vanilla, and salt. Gradually stir in flour. Shape dough into 2 rolls, each about 1½ inches in diameter and 6 inches long. Roll each in ¼ cup pecans to coat outside. Wrap in waxed paper; chill thoroughly. Cut into slices ¼ inch thick. Place on ungreased cookie sheet. Bake in moderate oven (350°) for 15 to 17 minutes, till lightly browned. Makes 4 dozen cookies.

Adult Birthday Party

ROAST ROCK CORNISH GAME HENS

Season four 1-pound ready-to-cook Cornish game hens inside and out with salt and pepper. Stuff each with ¼ cup stuffing, if desired. Place, breast up, on rack in shallow roasting pan and brush well with ⅓ cup melted butter. Roast loosely covered at 375° for 30 minutes, then 60 minutes uncovered or till done. During last 15 minutes of roasting, baste several times with mixture of ¼ cup canned condensed consomme and ¼ cup light corn syrup. Makes 4 servings.

BURNT-SUGAR CAKE

  ½ cup shortening
1½ cups sugar
  1 teaspoon vanilla
  2 eggs
2½ cups sifted cake flour
  3 teaspoons baking powder
    Burnt-sugar Syrup

Cream shortening and sugar till light. Add vanilla, then eggs, one at a time, beating 1 minute after each. Sift together dry ingredients and ½ teaspoon salt and add to creamed mixture alternately with ¾ cup water, beating smooth after each addition. Add 3 tablespoons Burnt-sugar Syrup. Beat thoroughly 4 minutes at medium speed on mixer.

Bake in 2 greased and lightly floured 9x1½-inch round pans at 375° about 20 minutes. (Or bake in two 8x1½-inch round pans at 350° for 25 to 30 minutes.) Cool 10 minutes; remove from pans. Cool. Fill with Date Filling and frost with Burnt-sugar Frosting.

BURNT-SUGAR SYRUP

Melt (caramelize) ⅔ cup granulated sugar in large heavy skillet, stirring constantly. When a deep golden brown syrup forms, remove from heat. Slowly add ⅔ cup boiling water. Heat and stir till all dissolves.

Boil to reduce syrup to ½ cup. Cool syrup before using. This is enough for both cake and frosting.

BURNT-SUGAR FROSTING

  2 egg whites
1¼ cups sugar
  3 to 4 tablespoons Burnt-sugar Syrup*
  ¼ cup cold water
  1 teaspoon vanilla

Place dash salt and all ingredients except vanilla in top of double boiler (not over heat); beat 1 minute with electric or rotary beater. Place over (but not touching) boiling water and cook, beating constantly, until mixture forms peaks, about 7 minutes (don't overcook). Remove from boiling water. Add vanilla and beat till of spreading consistency, about 2 minutes. Reserve ¼ cup frosting for Date Filling. Use remaining frosting on cake.

*If you have a sweet tooth, use only 3 tablespoons, if you like a "touch of bitter," try 4 tablespoons of Burnt-sugar Syrup.

DATE FILLING

In saucepan, combine 1½ cups pitted dates, cut up; 1 cup water; ⅓ cup sugar; and ¼ teaspoon salt. Bring to boiling. Cook and stir over low heat about 4 minutes or till thick. Remove from heat. Cool to room temperature. Fold in ¼ cup Burnt-sugar Frosting and ¼ cup chopped walnuts. Spread between cooled cake layers. Makes 1½ cups.

GREENGAGE PLUM SALAD

  1 30-ounce can greengage plums
  1 3-ounce package lemon-flavored gelatin
  1 3-ounce package lime-flavored gelatin
  1 cup finely chopped celery
  1 3-ounce package cream cheese, softened
  3 tablespoons light cream
  1 tablespoon mayonnaise

Drain plums, reserving syrup; sieve plums. Add water to syrup to make 3½ cups; heat. Add gelatins; stir to dissolve. Add plums.

Chill till partially set; fold in celery. Turn into 8x8x2-inch pan. Blend remaining ingredients. Spoon atop; swirl through to marble. Chill firm. Cut in 9 or 12 squares.

Shower Luncheon

BING CHERRY MOLD

2 3-ounce packages cherry- *or* black-
  cherry-flavored gelatin
2 teaspoons lemon juice
2 tablespoons sherry
1 cup dairy sour cream
2 cups halved, pitted, fresh
  dark sweet cherries
¼ cup chopped almonds, toasted

Dissolve gelatin in 2 cups boiling water; add 1 cup cold water and lemon juice. To *1 cup gelatin mixture* add the sherry; pour into an 8½-cup mold and chill till almost firm.

Meanwhile, chill remaining gelatin till partially set, then whip till fluffy; fold in sour cream, cherries, and almonds. Pour atop gelatin layer in mold. Chill till firm, about 5 hours or overnight.

Unmold on chilled platter. If desired, circle with fresh cherries, sliced pineapple, and romaine, and pass a mixture of dairy sour cream and mayonnaise. Serves 10 to 12.

CURRIED CHICKEN SANDWICHES

Arrange 8 slices buttered toast (trim crusts) on baking sheet; cover with 8 large slices or 3 cups cubed cooked chicken. Sprinkle with salt and pepper. Cut each sandwich in half diagonally. Mix 1½ cups mayonnaise, ⅔ cup finely chopped celery, ½ cup sliced green onions and tops, 1½ teaspoons curry powder, 1 teaspoon salt, and dash pepper. Spread over chicken to edges of toast. Bake at 375° for 15 minutes. Makes 8 servings.

WALNUT CREAM ROLL

4 egg whites
1 teaspoon vanilla
½ cup sugar
4 egg yolks
¼ cup sifted all-purpose flour
½ cup chopped walnuts
• • •
1 cup whipping cream
1 tablespoon sugar

Beat whites with ½ teaspoon salt and vanilla till soft peaks form. Gradually beat in ½ cup sugar till stiff peaks form. Beat yolks till thick and lemon colored. Fold yolks into whites; carefully fold in flour and nuts. Spread batter evenly in well-greased and floured 15½x10½x 1-inch jelly roll pan. Bake at 375° for 12 minutes or till done.

Immediately loosen sides of cake and turn out onto towel sprinkled with sifted confectioners' sugar. Starting at narrow end, roll cake and towel together; cool on rack. Whip cream with 1 tablespoon sugar till stiff. Unroll cake; spread with whipped cream. Reroll cake; chill. At serving time, top cake with additional whipped cream. Serves 8 to 10.

Dessert Shower

COFFEE CLOUDS

3 egg whites
1 teaspoon vanilla
1 teaspoon instant coffee powder
¼ teaspoon cream of tartar
1 cup sugar
1 6-ounce package (1 cup)
  butterscotch pieces
1 tablespoon instant coffee powder
1 beaten egg
1 cup whipping cream, whipped
  Shaved unsweetened chocolate

Shells: Beat egg whites with next 3 ingredients and dash salt till frothy. Add sugar, a small amount at a time, beating till stiff peaks form and sugar is dissolved. Cover cookie sheet with ungreased brown paper. Draw eight 3½-inch circles; spread each with ⅓ cup meringue. Shape with back of spoon to make shells. Bake at 275° for 1 hour. For crisper meringues, turn off heat; let dry in oven (door closed) about 1 hour. Cool.

Filling: Combine butterscotch pieces, 3 tablespoons water, 1 tablespoon instant coffee powder, and dash salt. Cook and stir over low heat till candy melts; cook 1 to 2 minutes longer. Stir small amount hot mixture into egg; return to hot mixture, cook and stir about 1 minute. Chill. Fold butterscotch mixture into whipped cream; pile into meringue shells. Chill several hours. Trim with shaved chocolate. Makes 8 servings.

DEMITASSE

Use 3 to 4 tablespoons coffee to 1 measuring cup water. Brew using any desired method. Serve hot in small cups. If desired, pass whipped cream and/or sugar.

Anniversary

ANNIVERSARY CAKE

You'll need to buy a set of round cake pans, 10x2, 8x2, and 6x2 inches—

    2 packages 2-layer-size white cake mix
    3 packages fluffy white frosting mix
    2½ to 3 cups sifted confectioners'
        sugar
    2 tablespoons butter, softened
        Few drops red food coloring

In large bowl, prepare both cake mixes at once according to package directions *increasing* mixing time to 6 minutes. Grease and flour three round cake pans (10x2-, 8x2-, and 6x2-inches). Fill pans half full. Bake at 350° until done, about 50 minutes for the 6-inch and 8-inch layers and 55 minutes for the 10-inch layer. Cool in pans 15 minutes; remove from pans and cool on rack.

Prepare frosting mixes according to package directions. Reserve 2 cups prepared frosting. Put layers together with frosting, then frost sides and tops smoothly. Allow to set. Blend the confectioners' sugar gradually into reserved frosting until of piping consistency. Blend in butter and food coloring.

With pastry tube, pipe swags and rosettes around cake. Top with anniversary symbol.

COCONUT-ICE CREAM BALLS

Make balls of 2 quarts vanilla ice cream, using medium (No. 20) scoop. Roll each ball in tinted* coconut (three 3-ounce cans or 3¾ cups flaked coconut), coating generously. Place on a foil-lined tray and freeze. Makes 24 to 28 balls.

*To tint coconut, add food coloring to 1 tablespoon water to reach desired color. Put coconut in jar, add colored water, cap jar; shake till tinted. Dry on paper towels.

PINK PUNCH

    ½ cup sugar
    1 cup fresh mint leaves or ¼ cup
        dried mint leaves
    2 10-ounce packages frozen
        raspberries
    2 6-ounce cans frozen pink-lemonade
        concentrate
        Raspberry sherbet (optional)

Combine sugar, mint leaves, and 2 cups boiling water; let stand 5 minutes. Add raspberries and concentrate; stir until thawed. Strain. Pour into punch bowl. Add 4 cups water. Chill thoroughly and serve over crushed ice. For trim, freeze part of punch mixture in ring mold and float atop punch. Deck ring with twists of lemon and sprigs of mint. If sherbet is used, pour in an additional 1 cup water. Float scoops of raspberry sherbet atop. Makes approximately 16 to 20 one-half cup servings.

Housewarming Party

SUBMARINE SANDWICHES

Brown giant brown-and-serve French rolls (about 8-inches long) according to package directions. Split rolls lengthwise, *but don't cut quite through.* Scoop out some of centers. Spread cut surfaces generously with prepared mustard, garlic butter, and/or mayonnaise with curry powder. Line bottoms of rolls with leaf lettuce. Pile on slices of corned beef, boiled ham, bologna, salami, pickled tongue, chicken, tuna, and herring as desired. Add slices of American and Swiss cheese, onion, olives, and dill pickle. Anchor sandwich with wooden picks. Make 1 per person.

TOFFEE BARS

Thoroughly cream 1 cup butter, 1 cup brown sugar, and 1 teaspoon vanilla. Add 2 cups sifted all-purpose flour; mix well. Stir in one 6-ounce package (1 cup) semi-sweet chocolate pieces and 1 cup chopped walnuts. Pat into ungreased 15½x10½x1-inch pan. Bake at 350° for 15 to 18 minutes. While warm, cut in bars. Cool. Makes 4 dozen bars.

Teen Special Occasion

HOT MULLED CIDER

2 quarts apple cider
½ cup brown sugar
¼ teaspoon salt
1 teaspoon whole allspice
1 teaspoon whole cloves
3 inches stick cinnamon

Combine cider, brown sugar, and salt. Tie spices in small piece of cheesecloth; add to cider. Cover; simmer slowly 20 minutes. Remove spices. Serve hot. If desired, float clove-studded orange slices atop. Serves 10.

SUGARED NUTS

Add 2 tablespoons cold water to 1 slightly beaten egg white. Stir in ½ cup sugar, ½ teaspoon salt, and ¼ teaspoon *each* ground cinnamon, ground cloves, and ground allspice. Mix well. Add 1 cup walnut halves and 1 cup blanched whole almonds; stir to coat. Place nuts, flat side down, on greased cookie sheet. Bake at 250° about 1 hour. Cool.

St. Patrick's Day

TOMATO REFRESHER

Perfect to whet the appetite—

Combine one 20-ounce can (2½ cups) tomato juice, 3 tablespoons lemon juice, 1 teaspoon sugar, 1 teaspoon Worcestershire sauce, and ¼ teaspoon celery salt. Chill. Stir. Makes five 4-ounce servings.

CHEESE STRAWS

Thoroughly cream ¼ cup butter with ¼ teaspoon bottled hot pepper sauce. Blend in ¾ cup shredded sharp process cheese, and ⅔ cup sifted flour. Chill 1 hour. On lightly floured surface, roll into 15x6-inch rectangle, ⅛-inch thick. Cut in strips 6x¾ inches. Bake on ungreased baking sheet at 350° for 10 to 12 minutes. Serve warm. Makes 20.

CORNED-BEEF DINNER

3 to 4 pound corned-beef brisket
2 onions, sliced
2 cloves garlic, minced
6 whole cloves
2 bay leaves

• • •

6 small to medium potatoes, pared
6 small carrots, pared
1 medium head cabbage, cut in 6 wedges

Place corned beef in Dutch oven and barely cover with hot water; add onions, garlic, cloves, and bay leaves. (If spices are purchased with corned beef, use in place of those listed above.) Cover and simmer (*do not boil*) 1 hour *per pound* of meat, or till fork tender. Remove meat from liquid and keep meat hot; add potatoes and carrots. Cover; bring to boiling and cook 10 minutes. Then add cabbage wedges; continue cooking 20 minutes longer or till vegetables are done.

To carve corned beef, cut at slight angle across the grain, making thin slices.

Spice Glaze: If you like, glaze the corned beef while vegetables cook. Spread fat side of meat lightly with prepared mustard. Then sprinkle with mixture of ¼ cup brown sugar and ¼ teaspoon ground cloves. Place in shallow pan. Bake in moderate oven (350°) 15 to 20 minutes or till nicely glazed.

BLARNEYSTONES

Turn cupcakes into Blarneystones. Make cupcakes from your favorite mix, according to package directions. Cool. Frost top and sides with fluffy frosting mix or 7-Minute Frosting. Cover with green-tinted coconut. (See how to tint coconut page 171.)

7-Minute Frosting: Combine 2 egg whites, 1½ cups sugar, 1½ teaspoons light corn syrup *or* ¼ teaspoon cream of tartar, ⅓ cup cold water, and dash salt in top of double boiler. Beat ½ minute with electric mixer to blend. Place over boiling water, but not touching water; beat constantly until frosting forms stiff peaks, about 7 minutes (don't overcook). Remove from boiling water. If desired, pour into mixing bowl. Add 1 teaspoon vanilla. Beat until of spreading consistency, about 2 minutes. Frost top and sides of cupcakes.

PERFECT POTATO SALAD

Seasonings and vinegar go directly on potato slices so sweet-sour flavors will be absorbed—

> 5 cups cubed, peeled, cooked potatoes
> 2 teaspoons sugar
> 1 teaspoon salt
> 1 teaspoon celery seed
> 2 teaspoons vinegar
> 1 cup chopped celery
> ½ cup chopped onion
> ½ cup chopped sweet pickle
> 1½ cups mayonnaise or salad dressing
> 4 hard-cooked eggs, sliced

Sprinkle potatoes with sugar, salt, celery seed, and vinegar. Add celery, onion, sweet pickle, and mayonnaise or salad dressing. Toss to mix. Fold in hard-cooked eggs.

Chill well. Serve in center of Tomato Aspic ring. Serve extra in bowl. Serves 8.

TOMATO ASPIC

To turn out loosen edges with knife, invert mold on platter, lay hot towel over mold, lift off—

> 2 envelopes (2 tablespoons)
>   unflavored gelatin
> 4 cups tomato juice
> ⅓ cup chopped onion
> ¼ cup chopped celery leaves
> 2 tablespoons brown sugar
> 1 teaspoon salt
> 2 small bay leaves
> 4 whole cloves
>   • • •
> 3 tablespoons lemon juice
>   • • •
> ½ to 1 cup finely chopped celery
> 2 tablespoons chopped green pepper

Soften gelatin in 1 *cup* cold tomato juice. In saucepan, combine 2 cups of the tomato juice with the onion, celery leaves, brown sugar, salt, bay leaves, and cloves. Simmer uncovered 5 minutes; strain.

Dissolve the softened gelatin in the *hot* tomato mixture. Add remaining tomato juice and the lemon juice. Chill till partially set. Fold in celery and green pepper. Pour into a 5½-cup ring mold. Chill firm, 5 to 6 hours or overnight. Makes 6 to 8 servings.

BACON CORNETTES

Dice 10 to 12 slices bacon, cook till crisp; drain. Sift together 1 cup sifted all-purpose flour, ¼ cup sugar, 4 teaspoons baking powder, and ¾ teaspoon salt; stir in 1 cup yellow cornmeal.

Add 2 eggs, 1 cup milk, and ¼ cup salad oil. Beat just till smooth, about 1 minute (do not overbeat). Stir in bacon. Fill greased muffin pans ⅔ full. Bake at 425° for 20 to 25 minutes. Makes about 1 dozen.

CHERRY CREME PARFAITS

Whip 1 cup whipping cream with 3 tablespoons sugar, 1 teaspoon vanilla, and dash salt. Fold in 1 cup dairy sour cream.

Alternate layers of whipped-cream mixture and one 21-ounce can cherry-pie filling (2½ cups) in parfait or sherbet glasses. Begin with a red layer and end with a white layer. Top each with a single cherry. Chill till serving time. Serves 8 to 10.

All-Occasion

AFTER-DINNER MOCHA

> 3 tablespoons sugar
> ¼ cup instant coffee powder
> 1 1-ounce square unsweetened
>   chocolate
> 3 cups milk

In saucepan, combine sugar, coffee, 1½ cups water, chocolate, and dash salt; stir over low heat till chocolate melts. Simmer 4 to 5 minutes, stirring occasionally. Gradually add milk; heat and stir till hot. Remove from heat and beat with rotary beater till frothy. Pour into cups; spoon dollop of whipped cream on each. Pass extra sugar and whipped cream. Makes 3 or 4 servings.

CHEESE BISQUE

To one 10¾-ounce can condensed Cheddar cheese soup, add 1 cup light cream and ⅓ cup sherry. Heat, stirring frequently. Serve in cups; sprinkle with popcorn. Serves 3 or 4.

Independence Day

HAWAIIAN HAM SLICES

Drain one 8½-ounce can sliced pineapple, reserving syrup; combine reserved syrup with 2 tablespoons soy sauce, ¾ teaspoon ground ginger, and ½ clove garlic. In shallow container, pour over 1 pound fully-cooked ham, cut into 4 slices. Marinate ham for 30 minutes, turning once. Discard garlic. Grill ham slices over hot coals just till heated through, about 2 minutes on each side. Brush with marinade once or twice. Heat pineapple slices on grill with ham last 2 minutes. To serve, top each slice ham with a pineapple slice. Makes 4 servings.

MACARONI AND CHEESE SALAD

      6 ounces shell macaroni
          (about 1½ cups)
      1 cup sliced celery
      1 cup shredded carrot
      ¼ cup chopped onion
      1 10¾-ounce can condensed
          Cheddar cheese soup
      ¼ cup salad oil
      2 tablespoons vinegar
      1 teaspoon sugar
      1 teaspoon prepared mustard
      1 teaspoon Worcestershire sauce

Cook macaroni according to package directions; drain and cool. Combine macaroni, celery, carrot, and onion. In small mixer bowl, combine condensed cheese soup, oil, vinegar, sugar, mustard, Worcestershire sauce, ½ teaspoon salt, and dash pepper; beat till well blended. Spoon atop macaroni mixture; mix well. Chill several hours. Serves 4 to 6.

DILLY FRENCH LOAF

Stir together ½ cup butter or margarine, softened, and ½ teaspoon dried dillweed. Slice 1 loaf French bread in 1-inch slices, *cutting to, but not through* bottom crust. Spread dill butter between slices; wrap loaf in heavy foil. Heat for 20 to 30 minutes on grill over low coals, turning frequently.

CARAMEL FROSTED BARS

      6 tablespoons butter or margarine
      ¾ cup sugar
      1 egg
      ¾ teaspoon vanilla
      1¼ cups sifted all-purpose flour
      ½ teaspoon soda
      ¼ cup chopped almonds, toasted
          Caramel Frosting

In bowl, cream together butter and sugar till light and fluffy. Beat in egg and vanilla. Sift together flour, soda, and ½ teaspoon salt. Add to creamed mixture; mix well. Stir in chopped almonds and spread in greased 9x9x 2-inch baking pan. Bake at 375° for 20 to 25 minutes. Cool slightly.

Prepare *Caramel Frosting:* In small saucepan, combine 2 tablespoons butter or margarine, ⅓ cup brown sugar, and 1 tablespoon water. Bring to a full boil; remove from heat. Add 1 teaspoon vanilla; gradually stir in 1 cup sifted confectioners' sugar. (If mixture is too thick, add a few drops hot water.) Spread *immediately* on slightly cooled baked layer; sprinkle with 2 tablespoons chopped toasted almonds. Cut into 24 bars.

Halloween

DOUBLE-CORN CHOWDER

      5 slices bacon
      1 12-ounce can (1½ cups) whole
          kernel corn
      1 medium onion, thinly sliced
      1 cup diced, pared raw potatoes
      1 10½-ounce can condensed cream of
          celery soup
      1¾ cups milk
      1 16-ounce can cream-style corn
          Butter or margarine

In large saucepan, cook bacon till crisp. Remove bacon, reserving drippings in pan. Drain whole kernel corn, reserving liquid. Add water to corn liquid to make ½ cup; add to drippings. Add onion, potatoes, and ½ teaspoon salt. Cover and simmer ¼ hour or till vegetables are tender. Add soup, milk, and corns; heat through. Season to taste. Crumble bacon over. Drop in butter pats. Serves 6 to 8.

CARAMEL APPLES ON STICKS

There's no greater fun for Halloween trick or treaters—

  1 14-ounce package (about 50)
     vanilla caramels
  2 tablespoons water
    Dash salt

       • • •

  6 wooden skewers

       • • •

  6 unpared crisp medium apples
    Chopped walnuts

Melt caramels with water in top of double boiler, stirring frequently, until smooth. Add salt. Insert a skewer into blossom end of each apple. Dip apple in caramel syrup and turn until bottom half of apple is completely coated. (If syrup is too stiff, add a few drops of water.)

At once roll bottom of coated apple in chopped nuts. Set on cookie sheet covered with waxed paper. Chill firm. Top sticks with corn candy, if desired.

Thanksgiving

OLD-TIME GIBLET GRAVY

In covered saucepan, simmer turkey giblets till tender in lightly salted water to cover—add a few celery leaves and onion slices if desired. Heart and gizzard take about 2 to 2½ hours—be sure they are fork tender. Liver takes 30 minutes; add it last half hour. Let giblets cool in broth; remove giblets and chop.

After transferring cooked turkey to a warm platter, leave crusty bits in pan and pour the liquid from pan into a large measuring cup. When fat comes to the top, skim it off. For *each cup of gravy* measure 2 tablespoons fat back into roasting pan. Add 2 tablespoons flour (per cup) and blend thoroughly.

Cook and stir over low heat till bubbly. Remove from heat and add 1 cup liquid (meat juices from roasting turkey plus giblet broth). Stir till smooth, return to heat and cook till thick and bubbly about 2 to 3 minutes, stirring constantly and scraping bottom and sides of pan to blend in crusty bits. Add chopped cooked giblets. Heat through. Season to taste.

HOT TOMATO BOUILLON

  1 10¾-ounce can condensed
     tomato soup
  1 10½-ounce can condensed
     beef broth
  ¼ teaspoon prepared horseradish
    Dash bottled hot pepper sauce
    Dairy sour cream

In saucepan, combine soup, broth, 1 cup water, horseradish, and pepper sauce. Simmer, uncovered, till heated through, about 5 minutes. Pour into serving dishes. Float spoonful of sour cream atop each. Makes 6 servings.

GOURMET ONIONS

  3 tablespoons butter or margarine
  ½ teaspoon monosodium glutamate
  ½ teaspoon sugar
  ¼ cup sherry
  10 to 12 small onions, peeled,
     cooked, and drained
  ¼ cup shredded Parmesan cheese

Melt butter in saucepan; stir in monosodium glutamate, sugar, ¼ teaspoon each salt and pepper, and sherry. Add onions and heat quickly about 5 minutes, stirring occasionally. Turn into serving dish and sprinkle with cheese. Makes 6 servings.

OYSTER STUFFING

  ½ cup chopped celery
  ½ cup chopped onion
  1 bay leaf
  ¼ cup butter or margarine
  6 cups dry bread crumbs
  1 tablespoon chopped parsley
  3 cups chopped raw oysters
  1 teaspoon poultry seasoning
  2 beaten eggs
  1¾ cups oyster liquor and milk

Cook celery, onion, and bay leaf in butter until celery and onion are tender but not brown. Discard bay leaf. Add crumbs and parsley; mix thoroughly. Add oysters, seasoning, salt and pepper to taste, and eggs. Add enough liquor mixture to moisten. Makes stuffing for a 10- to 12-pound turkey.

Holiday Dinner

CHRISTMAS CHEESE CHOWDER

½ cup shredded carrots
½ cup diced celery
1 13¾-ounce can (1¾ cups)
    chicken broth
¼ cup chopped onion
¼ cup chopped green pepper
3 tablespoons butter or margarine
3 tablespoons all-purpose flour
2 cups milk
4 ounces Gruyere cheese, shredded
    (1 cup)
4 ounces sharp process American
    cheese, shredded (1 cup)

Combine carrots, celery, and chicken broth; cover and simmer until tender. Cook onion and green pepper in butter until tender. Blend in flour; add milk all at once. Cook, stirring constantly, until mixture thickens and boils. Cook 2 minutes. Add broth mixture; heat to boiling. Reduce heat; add cheeses; stir till melted. Season. Serves 6 to 8.

FROZEN EGGNOG

¼ cup sugar
2 tablespoons all-purpose flour
2 cups milk
2 well-beaten egg yolks
2 cups dairy eggnog
1½ teaspoons vanilla
• • •
2 egg whites
¼ cup sugar

Combine ¼ cup sugar, flour, and ¼ teaspoon salt. Gradually stir in milk. Cook, stirring constantly, till thick. Stir small amount of hot mixture into egg yolks; return to hot mixture; cook and stir about 2 minutes. Stir in eggnog and vanilla. Pour into refrigerator tray and partially freeze. Turn into chilled mixing bowl and beat till smooth and fluffy with electric or rotary beater. Beat egg whites till soft peaks form; gradually add ¼ cup sugar, beating until stiff peaks form and sugar is dissolved. Quickly fold meringue into eggnog mixture. Return to tray and freeze till firm. Makes 6 to 8 servings.

BROCCOLI WITH EASY HOLLANDAISE

2 10-ounce packages frozen broccoli
    spears
½ cup dairy sour cream
½ cup mayonnaise or salad dressing
1 teaspoon prepared mustard
2 teaspoons lemon juice

Cook broccoli according to package directions. Meanwhile, combine sour cream, mayonnaise, mustard, and lemon juice in saucepan. Cook and stir over low heat until just heated through. Serve over broccoli. Makes 6 to 8 servings.

Trimming the Tree Party

CHILI CON CARNE

In a hurry? Make chili the day before and reheat—

2 pounds ground beef
2 large onions, chopped
2 green peppers, chopped
2 16-ounce cans tomatoes, broken up
2 8-ounce cans tomato sauce
2 16-ounce cans dark red
    kidney beans, drained
2 to 4 teaspoons chili powder
1½ teaspoons salt
1 bay leaf

In heavy skillet, cook meat, onion, and green pepper till meat is lightly browned and vegetables are tender. Stir in remaining ingredients. Cover and simmer for 1 hour. Remove bay leaf. Makes 8 servings.

STUFFED CELERY

1 5-ounce jar smoky cheese spread
1 2¼-ounce can deviled ham
2 tablespoons sweet pickle relish
⅛ teaspoon salt
1 teaspoon Dijon-style mustard
    Celery stalks

Thoroughly combine all ingredients except celery. Stuff into celery stalk sections. Makes about 1 cup filling.

CRISP CHEESE TRIANGLES

2 tablespoons butter or margarine
2 ounces Liederkranz cheese
Dash paprika
Dash dry mustard
6 slices white bread

Cream together butter or margarine, cheese, paprika, and dry mustard. Spread 1 tablespoon of the mixture on one side of each bread slice. Cut each slice into 4 triangles. Bake on baking sheet at 350° for 20 minutes or till golden brown. Makes 24 triangles.

CHRISTMAS LIME PARFAIT PIE

2 3-ounce packages or 1 6-ounce package lime-flavored gelatin
2 cups boiling water
1 teaspoon shredded lime peel
⅓ cup lime juice
1 quart vanilla ice cream
1 baked 10-inch pastry shell

Dissolve gelatin in boiling water. Stir in lime peel and juice. Add ice cream by spoonfuls, stirring till melted. Chill till mixture mounds. Pile into pastry shell. Chill till firm. Top with whipped cream and maraschino cherries. Makes 8 servings.

PASTRY

1½ cups sifted all-purpose flour
½ cup shortening
4 to 5 tablespoons cold water

Sift together flour and ½ teaspoon salt; cut in shortening with pastry blender or blending fork till pieces are the size of small peas. Sprinkle 1 tablespoon water over part of mixture. Gently toss with fork; push to side of bowl. Sprinkle next tablespoon water over dry part; mix lightly; push to moistened part at side. Repeat till all is moistened. Form into ball. Flatten on lightly floured surface. Roll from center to edge till ⅛-inch thick. Fit pastry into pie plate, trim ½ to 1 inch beyond center; fold under and flute. Prick bottom and sides with fork. Bake in very hot oven (450°) for 10 to 12 minutes or till golden.

EGGNOG

⅓ cup sugar
2 egg yolks
¼ teaspoon salt
4 cups milk
•   •   •
2 egg whites
3 tablespoons sugar
1 teaspoon vanilla
Brandy or rum flavoring to taste

Beat ⅓ cup sugar into egg yolks. Add salt; stir in milk. Cook over medium heat, stirring constantly till mixture coats a metal spoon. Cool to room temperature.

Beat egg whites till foamy. Gradually add the 3 tablespoons sugar, beating till soft peaks form. Fold egg whites, vanilla, and flavorings into custard mixture. Chill 3 or 4 hours. Sprinkle individual servings with freshly ground nutmeg, if desired. Makes 8 servings.

Holiday Open House

Perky red and green for the holidays—

PINWHEEL SANDWICHES

1 loaf unsliced sandwich bread
•   •   •
½ pound (1 cup) braunschweiger
¼ teaspoon dried dillweed
¼ cup mayonnaise or salad dressing
•   •   •
1 cup chopped watercress
2 3-ounce packages cream cheese, softened
Dash salt

Remove crusts from bread and slice lengthwise, ⅜-inch thick. (This may be done at the bakery.)
For Braunschweiger filling: Blend braunschweiger, dillweed, and mayonnaise.
For Watercress filling: Blend watercress, cream cheese, and salt.
To assemble sandwiches, spread ¼ cup of desired filling on each bread slice. Beginning at narrow end, roll up in pinwheel fashion. Wrap each roll in foil; chill thoroughly. Slice each roll to make 6 sandwiches. Makes about 4 dozen small sandwiches.

HAM NUGGETS

½ pound ground fully-cooked ham
½ pound ground fresh pork
¼ cup chopped green onions with tops
1 5-ounce can water chestnuts,
    drained and finely chopped
1 slightly beaten egg
1 tablespoon milk
1 small clove garlic, crushed

Thoroughly mix all ingredients. Using about 2 teaspoons meat mixture for each, form in marble-size meatballs. Brown slowly on all sides in small amount of hot shortening. Continue cooking, turning frequently, till meat is cooked through. Serve hot, with wooden picks for spearing. Makes about 5 dozen.

DEVILED HAM DIP

2 4½-ounce cans deviled ham
1 8-ounce package cream cheese,
    softened
1 tablespoon catsup
1 to 2 teaspoons finely chopped
    onion
2 tablespoons chopped pimiento-
    stuffed green olives

Combine all ingredients; chill till served. Garnish with additional chopped stuffed olives, if desired. Serve with crackers. Makes about 2 cups dip.

COFFEE ROYAL EGGNOG

1 quart dairy or canned eggnog,
    well chilled
1 pint vanilla ice cream,
    softened
2 to 3 teaspoons instant coffee
    powder
½ teaspoon rum flavoring

. . .

Whipping cream, whipped
Ground nutmeg

Combine eggnog, ice cream, coffee powder, and rum flavoring; blend thoroughly. Pour into punch bowl or chilled cups; top with whipped cream and dash of nutmeg. Makes 10 to 12 servings.

MINCEMEAT TURNOVERS

1 stick piecrust mix
½ cup prepared mincemeat
    Milk
    Sugar
    Sharp Cheddar cheese, cut in
        ¾-inch cubes

Prepare piecrust according to package directions; roll out. Cut in 3-inch circles. Place about 1 teaspoon mincemeat on one half of each circle. On other half, gently press tiny star cutter. (Make only impression; do not remove cut star from pastry.) Fold pastry, forming half circles. Seal edges with fork. Brush with milk; sprinkle with sugar. Bake at 400° for 10 to 12 minutes or till golden brown. Garnish with cheese cubes. Makes 1½ dozen.

NOEL FRUIT BARS

2 eggs
1 cup sifted confectioners' sugar
¼ cup butter or margarine, melted
¾ cup sifted all-purpose flour
1½ teaspoons baking powder
1 cup chopped walnuts
1 cup snipped dates
¾ cup chopped mixed candied fruits

Beat eggs till light and fluffy; gradually beat in confectioners' sugar. Stir in melted butter. Sift together dry ingredients and ½ teaspoon salt. Fold into egg mixture with nuts and fruits. Spread in greased 9x9x2-inch baking pan. Bake at 325° for 30 to 35 minutes. Cut in bars; frost with butter frosting and top with candied cherries, if desired. Makes about 1½ dozen.

Christmas Eve Supper

TOMATO CHICKEN-RICE COMBO

2 10¾-ounce cans condensed cream of tomato soup
1 10½-ounce can condensed chicken-rice soup
1½ soup cans milk

Combine all ingredients in saucepan. Cook and stir till heated through. Serves 4 or 5.

Holiday Breakfast

SWISS BAKED EGGS

4 slices bacon
4 tablespoons light cream
4 tablespoons shredded process Swiss cheese

. . .

4 eggs
2 teaspoons snipped chives

Cook bacon until crisp; drain. In each of four ramekins, crumble 1 slice bacon; add 1 tablespoon cream and 1 tablespoon Swiss cheese. Break 1 egg into each ramekin. Sprinkle with salt and pepper.

Set cups in shallow baking dish; pour hot water around cups to depth of 1 inch. Bake in a slow oven (325°) 15 to 20 minutes. Sprinkle each egg with ½ teaspoon snipped chives and 1 tablespoon cheese. Bake until eggs are set, about 15 minutes longer. Makes 4 servings.

CHRISTMAS MORGEN BROT

1 package active dry yeast
⅔ cup milk, scalded
6 tablespoons shortening
⅓ cup sugar
½ teaspoon salt

. . .

1 beaten egg
12 drops almond extract
¼ teaspoon ground cardamom
3 to 3½ cups sifted all-purpose flour
¼ cup light raisins

. . .

2 tablespoons butter or margarine, melted
½ cup sugar
1 tablespoon ground cinnamon
¼ teaspoon ground nutmeg

. . .

1 cup sifted confectioners' sugar
1 tablespoon hot water
1½ teaspoons butter or margarine

Soften yeast in ¼ cup warm water (110°). Combine hot milk, shortening, sugar, and salt; cool to lukewarm. Stir in softened yeast, egg, extract, and cardamom. Add *half* of the flour and beat until smooth. Add raisins and enough of the remaining flour to make a soft dough. Turn out on lightly floured surface; knead till smooth and satiny (about 8 to 10 minutes). Place in lightly greased bowl, turning once to grease surface. Cover and let rise in warm place till double (1 to 1½ hours).

Cut off ⅔ of dough. Divide into thirds and roll each portion into 12x5-inch rectangle. Brush with 4 teaspoons melted butter.

Combine ½ cup sugar, cinnamon, and nutmeg. Sprinkle 2 tablespoons of the mixture on each rectangle. Starting at long edge, roll each as for jelly roll; seal. Braid the three rolls together; seal ends; place on greased baking sheet.

To make second braid, divide remaining dough into thirds and roll each portion into 12x3-inch rectangle. Brush with remaining 2 teaspoons melted butter. Sprinkle with remaining sugar mixture. Roll and braid as before. Lay small braid on top of large braid; tuck in ends. Let rise in warm place till double (about 1 hour). Bake at 350° for 20 to 25 minutes. While warm, frost with a glaze made by blending confectioners' sugar with hot water and 1½ teaspoons butter.

PLANNING FOR A CROWD

Foods	Servings	Serving Unit	Amount to Purchase
BEVERAGES			
Coffee, ground	40 to 50	¾ cup	1 pound (5 cups)
Milk	24	1 cup	1½ gallons
Tea, instant, iced	40	¾ cup	1 cup
Tea, leaves	50	¾ cup	1 cup
DESSERTS			
Cake	24	2½-inch squares	1 15½x10½x1-inch sheet cake
Ice cream	24	½ cup or 1 slice	3 quarts
Pie	30	⅙ of pie	5 9-inch pies
FRUIT			
Canned	24	½ cup	1 6½- to 7½-lb. can
MEAT			
Beef roast, chuck	25	4 ounces	12¼ pounds, bone in
Ground beef	25	3-ounce patty	6¾ pounds
Ham, baked, sliced	25	4 ounces	10 pounds, boneless
Chicken	24	¼ chicken	6 chickens
Turkey	25	3 ounces	15 pounds
PASTA, RICE			
Rice, long-grain	24	½ cup, cooked	1½ pounds uncooked
Spaghetti and noodles	25	¾ cup, cooked	2½ pounds uncooked
RELISHES (combine several)			
Carrot strips	25	2-3 strips	1 pound
Celery	25	1 2- to 3-inch piece	1 pound
Olives	25	3 to 4 olives	1 quart
Pickles	25	1 ounce	1 quart
SALADS			
Fruit	24	⅓ cup	2 quarts
Potato	24	½ cup	3 quarts
Tossed Vegetable	25	¾ cup	5 quarts
Salad dressing	32	1 tablespoon	1 pint
SOUP	25	1 cup (**main course**)	1½ gallons or 10 10½- to 11-ounce cans condensed or 2 50-ounce cans condensed
VEGETABLES			
Canned	28	½ cup	4 1-lb. 11 ounce to 1 lb. 13-ounce cans
	25	½ cup	1 6½ to 7¼ lb. cans
Fresh:			
Lettuce, for salad, Iceberg	24	⅙ head, raw	4 heads
Onions	25	⅓ cup, small whole or pieces	6¼ pounds
Potatoes, mashed	24	½ cup, mashed	6 pounds, raw
Frozen:			
Beans, green or wax	25	⅓ cup	5¼ pounds
Carrots	25	⅓ cup, sliced	5 pounds
Corn, whole kernel	25	⅓ cup	5 pounds
Peas	25	⅓ cup	5 pounds
Potatoes, French fried	25	10 pieces	3¼ pounds

WINES AND COCKTAILS

The use of wine and cocktails in entertaining is a very personal choice. Many feel that a dinner is not complete without the complement of the appropriate wine, or the finale of a fine liqueur. Today no book on entertaining would be complete without the inclusion of the use of wine and spirits. This section is intended to serve as a basic guide in the use of wines and the mixing of party beverages. Additional reference material is listed on page 192.

Appetizer Wines

Foods to serve with them: these wines, being appetizers themselves, do not require food to be served with them. However, they are generally compatible with all appetizer foods. Serve appetizer wines chilled to a temperature of approximately 40-45 degrees.

Types to serve: Sherry, especially dry varieties; Vermouth, both dry and sweet; and the so-called flavored wines.

Red Table Wines

Foods to serve with them: all red meats including steaks, stews, roasts; game, goose, duck; veal and cheese. (White Wine can also be served with the latter two.) Except for Rose, which should be served at 45-50 degrees, serve all other red table wines at 60-70 degrees.

Types to serve: Claret or Cabernet Sauvignon; Burgundy or Pinot Noir; Rose; Beaujolais or Gamay; Red Chianti; and Zinfandel.

White Table Wines

Foods to serve with them: chicken, turkey (red wine also suitable), poultry of all kinds; Fish and shellfish; Ham; Veal (light red wine also goes with veal).

Types to serve: Rhine or Riesling; Graves; Moselle; Pouilly-Fuisse; Pinot Chardonnay or White Burgundy; Chablis; and Sauterne (especially the drier varieties).

Dessert Wines

Foods to serve with them: Fruit, nuts, cakes, some dessert cheeses.

Types to serve: Port, either Ruby or Tawny; White Tokay, Cream or Sweet Sherry; Sweet Madeira; Sauterne (the less dry varieties).

Sparkling Wines

Foods to serve: The sparkling wines are suitable with almost all foods and occasions. Refrigerate one to two hours to chill.

Types to serve: Sparkling Burgundy; Sparkling Rose; Champagnes either gold or pink (Brut is very dry, Sec semi-dry, and Demi-Sec less dry).

After Dinner Wines

Types to serve: Port; Cognac or Brandy; Calvados.

General tips

Sweet wines shouldn't be served with main dishes.
Red wines shouldn't be served with fish.
Red wines and after dinner wines should be served at 60-70 degrees (or what was regarded as "room temperature" before central heating).
Red wines should be uncorked an hour or more before serving.
Let your own taste, not someone else's, be your guide.

There are many tools available for the preparing of mixed drinks. An adequate bar set should consist of an ice bucket, tongs, corkscrew, shaker-strainer, shot glass, ice crusher, shaker, pitcher, stirring rod or spoon, measuring spoons, and cutting board and knife.

For the best results in mixing the cocktail, follow your recipes exactly as written using fresh fruit juices and peels, chilled or frosted glasses, shaved or chopped ice, and the right size and shape glass whenever called for.

Equivalents: 1 dash = 1/6 teaspoon; 1 teaspoon = ⅛ ounce; 1 tablespoon = ½ ounce; 1 pony = 1 ounce; 1 jigger = 1½ ounces; 8 ounces = 1 cup.

Servings: 1 pint = 16 ounces = 8 to 10 servings; 1 fifth = 25.6 ounces = 12 to 16 servings; 1 quart = 32 ounces = 16 to 20 servings; 1 bottle wine = 25.6 ounces = 4 to 8 servings; 1 split champagne or wine = 6.4 ounces = 2 servings; 1 half bottle = 12.8 ounces = 4-5 servings; 1 quart champagne = 26 ounces = 6 to 8 servings.

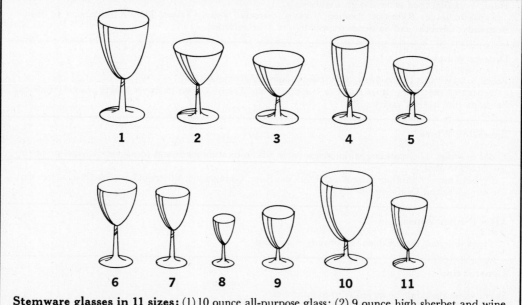

Unfooted beverage set in six sizes: (1) 7½ ounce old-fashioned cocktail; (2) 12 ounce double old-fashioned or other tall drinks (Tom Collins); (3) 12 ounce highball; (4) 9 ounce scotch and soda; (5) 5 ounce whiskey sour or other short cocktail; (6) 1½ ounce jigger (whiskey).

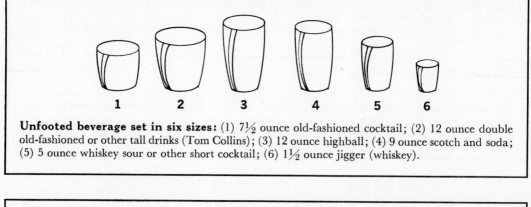

Stemware glasses in 11 sizes: (1) 10 ounce all-purpose glass; (2) 9 ounce high sherbet and wine glass; (3) 7 to 8 ounce low sherbet and wine glass; (4) 6 ounce whiskey sour or pilsner glass; (5) 4 ounce cocktail (martini) glass; (6) 5 ounce claret for red wines; (7) 4 ounce wine (white) or brandy glass; (8) 1 ounce cordial for liqueurs; (9) 4½ ounce sherry glass; (10) 15 ounce luncheon goblet; (11) 5 ounce orange juice or liqueur glass.

Party Punches

BURGUNDY PUNCH

2 fifths Burgundy
2 cups port wine
2 cups orange juice
¼ cup lemon juice
1 cup sugar
1 quart water
2 quarts ice

Combine Burgundy, port, orange juice, and lemon juice. Stir in sugar and water and mix well. Chill till serving time. Just before serving, pour over 2 quarts ice cubes (3 to 4 trays) in punch bowl. Makes about 4 quarts.

MULLED WINE

1 bottle (4/5 quart) claret wine
¼ cup sugar
   Peel from ½ lemon
   Peel from ½ orange
3 inches stick cinnamon
¼ teaspoon ground nutmeg
6 whole cloves
   • • •
   Thin orange slices

In saucepan, combine claret, sugar, lemon and orange peel (white membrane removed), cinnamon stick, nutmeg, and cloves. Simmer uncovered, very gently for 5 minutes. Strain and serve hot. Garnish with thin orange slices. Makes approximately 8 servings.

SANGRIA DE GUADALAJARA

¾ cup light corn syrup
⅓ cup lemon juice
   Few drops red food coloring
2 cups sparkling water
   • • •
2 cups port wine

Blend together corn syrup, lemon juice, and food coloring; stir in sparkling water. Divide mixture among 4 tall glasses. Add ice cubes, then carefully pour ½ cup of the wine down the side of the glass. Insert straws and serve. Makes 4 servings.

FIRETONG PUNCH

1 bottle (about 3¼ cups) dry
   red wine
¾ cup granulated sugar
3 whole cloves
½ cup orange juice
¼ cup lemon juice
3x1½-inch strip orange peel
2x½-inch strip lemon peel
½ cup sugar cubes
¼ cup rum, heated
   Orange slices

Heat wine with granulated sugar, cloves, fruit juices, and peels. Do not boil. Pour into flame-proof punch bowl. Soak sugar cubes in rum; place cubes in a strainer over punch. Ignite sugar cubes; as they flame, gradually spoon more heated rum from a long-handled ladle over the cubes. When sugar has all melted into punch, add a few orange slices. Serve hot in small cups. Makes 8 servings.

FROSTED FRUIT PUNCH

½ cup sugar
½ cup water
2 inches stick cinnamon
3 whole cloves
1 pint (2 cups) sauterne
1 12-ounce can (1¼ cups) apple juice
1 cup orange juice
¼ cup lemon juice
   • • •
1 pint orange sherbet

Combine sugar, water, cinnamon, and cloves. Bring to boiling; reduce heat and simmer, uncovered, 5 minutes. Strain and cool. Stir in all ingredients except sherbet and chill thoroughly. Serve in iced-tea glasses or place in small punch bowl; top with spoonfuls of orange sherbet. Makes 6 servings.

ROSE FRAPPE

1 bottle (4/5 quart) rose wine
1 6-ounce can frozen lemonade
¾ cup water

Combine all ingredients. Pour over crushed ice. Makes 8 servings.

CHAMPAGNE COCKTAIL

4/5 pint (1¾ cups) champagne
2 cups ginger ale
1 cup orange juice
Strawberries, rinsed, hulled,
and sliced

Chill ingredients; mix together in large pitcher. Serve in small glasses with a few strawberry slices in each. Serves 8 to 10.

ROSY WASSAIL

1 pint cranberry juice cocktail
1 6-ounce can frozen orange juice
concentrate, thawed
1 tablespoon sugar
¼ teaspoon ground allspice
1 bottle (about 3¼ cups) sauterne
Thick orange slices
Whole cloves

In large kettle, combine first four ingredients and 2 cups water; bring almost to simmering. Add sauterne and heat through, but do not boil. If desired, stir in a few drops red food coloring. Stud orange slices with cloves. Pour punch into preheated bowl; float orange slices atop. Makes 12 to 14 servings.

WARREN'S GLUGG

2 quarts apple juice
3 sticks cinnamon, broken
1 tablespoon whole cloves
Dash ground nutmeg
½ pound white raisins
4 cardamom buds*
1½ oranges, sliced and quartered
1 fifth dark rum
1 fifth brandy

Combine first 6 ingredients. Let stand 12 to 24 hours. Before serving, pour mixture into kettle and bring to boiling; reduce heat and simmer 30 minutes. Add orange pieces; reheat till heated through. Add rum and brandy. Serve immediately from kettle over low heat. Makes about 24 punch cup servings.

*Use seeds only from buds; shell and crush seeds between 2 tablespoons or in mortar and pestle; steep in 2 or 3 tablespoons water.

Cocktails

BLOODY MARY

Combine and shake in a cocktail shaker 2 jiggers (3 ounces) tomato juice, 1 jigger (1½ ounces) vodka, the juice from half a lemon, dash Worcestershire sauce, celery salt and pepper to taste, and chopped ice. Strain into a 6-ounce cocktail glass.

For a variation, add clam juice to taste. Garnish with a thin lemon slice.

BRANDY ALEXANDER

In a cocktail shaker, shake 1 ounce creme de cacao, 1 tablespoon heavy cream, 1 ounce brandy, and 3 or 4 ice cubes. Strain and serve in 4-ounce cocktail glass.

BULLSHOT

Combine 3 or 4 ice cubes, 2 jiggers (3 ounces) vodka, and ½ cup cold bouillon in a mixing glass. Add salt and pepper to taste and stir. Strain into a chilled glass.

COLLINS

Shake well 1 jigger vodka or gin, 1½ teaspoons superfine sugar, and juice from ½ lemon. Pour into ice-filled highball glass and add club soda to fill. Garnish with an orange slice and maraschino cherry if desired.

DAIQUIRI

Combine ½ jigger lime juice, 1 jigger (1½ ounces) light rum, powdered sugar to taste, 1 teaspoon Triple Sec (optional), and crushed ice in a shaker. Shake well and strain into a stemmed cocktail glass.

GIMLET

Combine 1 jigger (1½ ounces) gin, vodka, or rum, ½ jigger lime juice, powdered sugar to taste, and cracked ice in a cocktail shaker. Shake well and strain into a cocktail glass.

GRASSHOPPER

Shake in a cocktail shaker 1 jigger (1½ ounces) creme de cacao, 1 jigger creme de menthe, 1 tablespoon heavy cream, and 3 or 4 ice cubes. Strain into a cocktail glass.

HIGHBALL

In a highball glass, combine 2 or 3 ice cubes, 2 ounces Scotch, rye, or bourbon. Fill with water, club soda, or ginger ale. Stir.

HOT BUTTERED RUM

In an old-fashioned glass, combine a piece stick cinnamon, 1 teaspoon sugar, a slice lemon peel, and 2 jiggers rum. Fill with boiling water; float a pat of butter atop.

HOT TODDY

Combine 2 jiggers whiskey, 1 teaspoon sugar, 2 or 3 whole cloves, and short piece stick cinnamon in a mug. Fill to top with boiling water and sprinkle with nutmeg. Garnish with lemon or lime slice if desired.

MANHATTAN

Traditional: Combine 1 jigger sweet vermouth with 2 or 2½ jiggers bourbon or rye, a dash of bitters, and cracked ice. Stir and strain into a chilled cocktail glass. Serve with a maraschino cherry.

Dry Manhattan: Substitute dry vermouth for sweet vermouth and serve with an olive.

Manhattan On-The-Rocks: Mix either of the above two recipes, then pour over 2 or 3 ice cubes placed in an old-fashioned glass.

MARGARITA

Moisten the rim of a stemmed cocktail glass with a slice of lemon or lime. Dip rim into salt. Shake together 1 jigger Tequila, 1½ tablespoons sugar or ½ ounce Triple Sec, 1 ounce fresh lemon or lime juice, and 3 to 4 ice cubes. Strain into rim-salted glass. If desired, garnish with either a lemon or lime slice.

MARTINI

Traditional: Combine ½ jigger dry vermouth, 1 jigger dry gin or vodka, and cracked ice. Stir and strain into a chilled cocktail glass. Add a lemon twist or an olive. For a Gibson, add a pearl onion instead of the olive.

Dry Martini: 5 parts dry gin or vodka, 1 part dry vermouth.

Extra Dry Martini: 7 parts dry gin or vodka (if only extra dry, not extra strong, use 80-proof), and 1 part dry vermouth.

OLD-FASHIONED

Crush ½ lump sugar, a dash or two of bitters, and drop cold water in an old-fashioned glass. Stir till sugar is dissolved. Add 2 ice cubes and 1 or 2 jiggers bourbon, Scotch, or rye and stir. If desired, add an orange slice or maraschino cherry.

SCREWDRIVER

Place 2 or 3 ice cubes and 2 jiggers vodka in highball glass. Fill with orange juice; stir. Decorate with an orange slice or a cherry.

SINGAPORE SLING

Combine cracked ice, ½ ounce cherry-flavored brandy, ½ ounce lemon juice, 1 teaspoon powdered sugar, and 1½ to 2 jiggers gin in a highball glass. Fill with cold or carbonated water, stir, decorate with fruits and serve with straws.

TONIC

Combine the juice and rind of ¼ lime, 1 jigger gin, vodka, or Tequila, and ice cubes in a tall glass. Fill with tonic water. Stir.

WHISKEY SOUR

Combine ½ jigger fresh lemon or lime juice, 2 jiggers bourbon, Scotch, or rye, 1 teaspoon powdered sugar, and 3 or 4 ice cubes. Shake well, strain into a glass. If desired, decorate with a lemon slice and a cherry.

Party equipment: left to right—automatic coffee maker; ice maker; wine cooler; steak knives; beverage glasses; fondue pot and forks; electric Dutch oven; large ashtray; electric rotisserie and grill; coasters; carving set. On hot-plate serving cart, top: percolator; patio pottery; large casserole; cordial glasses; bar knife and opener; bottom: electric bun warmer; napkins; bar set of tongs, opener, spoon, corkscrew, muddler, strainer, double shot glass.

INDEX

I

J-K-L

M

N

O-P

R

S

T-U-V

W-X-Y-Z

CREDITS

Bibliography

Wines

Lichine, Alexis, *Encyclopedia of Wines and Spirits*, Knopf, c1967
Lichine, Alexis, *Wines of France*, Knopf, c1963
Misch, Robert J., *Quick Guide to Wine*, Doubleday, c1966
Schoonmaker, Frank, *Encyclopedia of Wine*, Hastings House, c1964
Simon, Andre L., *Noble Grapes and the Great Wines of France*, McGraw-Hill, c1957
Simon, Andre L., *Wines of the World*, McGraw-Hill, c1967
Waugh, Alec, *Wines and Spirits*, Time-Life Books, c1968

Games

Bell, Robert Charles, *Board and Table Games*, Oxford University Press, c1960
Burns, Lorell Coffman, *Instant Party Fun*, Association Press, c1967
Eisenberg, Helen, *The Omnibus of Fun*, Association Press, c1956
Morehead, Albert Hodges, *The New Complete Hoyle*, Garden City Books, c1964
Mulae, Margaret E., and Holmes, Marian S., *The Party Game Book*, Harper and Row, c1951
Thomsen, R., *Games, Anyone?*, Doubleday, c1964

Photographs

National Design Center

Owens-Corning Fiberglas, pp. 106, 116
Celanese Corporation, p. 109
Sterling Silversmiths Guild of America, p. 111

Potted Plant Information Center, pp. 112, 115
Reed and Barton Flatware, p. 113
Fostoria Glassware, p. 113

Party Equipment Manufacturers (pp. 186-187)

Automatic coffee maker: The West Bend Company, West Bend, Wisconsin
Ice maker: U-Line Corporation, Milwaukee, Wisconsin
Steak knives: Ekco Housewares Company, Franklin Park, Illinois
Beverage glasses: Fostoria Glass Company, Moundsville, West Virginia
Wine Cooler: Towle Manufacturing Company, Newburyport, Massachusetts
Electric Dutch oven: The West Bend Company, West Bend, Wisconsin
Electric rotisserie and grill, The West Bend Co., West Bend, Wisconsin
Coasters: Lunt Silversmiths, Greenfield, Massachusetts
Carving Set: The International Silver Company, Meriden, Connecticut
Patio pottery: Taylor Smith and Taylor Company, Chester, West Virginia
Dutch oven: Corning Glass Works, Corning, New York
Cordial glasses: Lunt Silversmiths, Greenfield, Massachusetts
Bar knife and opener: Lunt Silversmiths, Greenfield, Massachusetts
Electric bun warmer: Salton, Inc., New York, New York
Bar set: Ekco Housewares Company, Franklin Park, Illinois
Serving cart: Salton, Inc., New York, New York

Designers
Robert Winquist, pp. 6, 49
Penny Butler, p. 48

Editorial Scouts
Barbara Lenox
Joanne Young